'I'm delighted to recommend W
Mainstone-Cotton for anyone int
Years wellbeing. This new book
into understandable and useful ins
practical advice, making it valuabl
alike. It's a heartfelt invitation to
aspect of our interactions with children.

Sonia uses examples from her own experience, like her morning coffee ritual and using clay in play schemes, to show how wellbeing practices can be integrated into daily life AND professional practice. These examples not only demonstrate effective strategies for supporting children's emotional health but also make the content relatable and actionable. The two-part structure of the book makes it useful both as a 'dip in and out' book and an accessible read from beginning to end.

This book is an essential read that I wholeheartedly endorse, brimming with wisdom, warmth, and a deep understanding of what it means to truly nurture wellbeing.'

Kathy Brodie, *Early Childhood Studies Lecturer*

Wellbeing Explained

Nurturing children and supporting their wellbeing is vitally important, along with looking after the wellbeing of the staff who support them. *Wellbeing Explained* highlights the importance of wellbeing and explains key terms associated with wellbeing and mental health needs. Unpicking terms such as holistic development, self-esteem, SEMH, and anxiety, it uses practical examples and case studies to explain what these mean and how we can promote wellbeing through policy and practices.

Divided into two parts, the first provides a brief overview of the key terms associated with wellbeing in early childhood alongside examples of what they mean in practice. Part two then shares the principles that underpin promoting good wellbeing, such as prioritising staff wellbeing, adopting a loving pedagogy, keeping the child and family central to provision, and creating an enabling environment explaining the underlying ethos of a child-centred approach.

Part of the *Key Concepts in Early Childhood Series*, this is essential reading for early years practitioners and students who want to know and understand what they can do to support their own wellbeing and the children they work with.

Sonia Mainstone-Cotton currently works with *Brighter Futures*, a specialist team supporting 3- and 4-years-olds who have social, emotional, and mental health needs. She delivers training on children's SEMH and wellbeing and has written 11 books.

Key Concepts of Early Childhood

Series Editor: Tamsin Grimmer

This exciting new series unpicks key terms and concepts in early childhood education and shows how they relate to everyday practice. Each book focuses on a core theme and provides clear, concise definitions of key terminology alongside case studies and then explores how these link to core areas of provision.

Wellbeing Explained
Sonia Mainstone-Cotton

Loving Pedagogy Explained
Tamsin Grimmer

Early Childhood Theorists and Approaches Explained
Chloe Webster

For more information about this series, please visit: Key Concepts in Early Childhood - Book Series - Routledge & CRC Press

Wellbeing Explained

Sonia Mainstone-Cotton

Routledge
Taylor & Francis Group

LONDON AND NEW YORK

Designed cover image: © Getty Images

First edition published 2025
by Routledge
4 Park Square, Milton Park, Abingdon, Oxon, OX14 4RN

and by Routledge
605 Third Avenue, New York, NY 10158

Routledge is an imprint of the Taylor & Francis Group, an informa business

© 2025 Sonia Mainstone-Cotton

British Library Cataloguing-in-Publication Data
A catalogue record for this book is available from the British Library

Library of Congress Cataloging-in-Publication Data
Names: Mainstone-Cotton, Sonia, author.
Title: Wellbeing explained / Sonia Mainstone-Cotton.
Description: First edition. | Abingdon, Oxon ; New York, NY : Routledge, 2025. |
   Series: Key concepts in early childhood | Includes bibliographical references.
Identifiers: LCCN 2024026729 (print) | LCCN 2024026730 (ebook) |
   ISBN 9781032692913 (hardback) | ISBN 9781032692838 (paperback) |
   ISBN 9781032692944 (ebook other)
Subjects: LCSH: Early childhood education—Great Britain. | Early childhood education—
   Psychological aspects. | Preschool children—Psychology. | Early childhood teachers—
   Psychology. | Child mental health—Great Britain. | Well-being—Great Britain.
Classification: LCC LB1139.3.G7 M25 2025 (print) | LCC LB1139.3.G7 (ebook) |
   DDC 372.210941—dc23/eng/20240802
LC record available at https://lccn.loc.gov/2024026729
LC ebook record available at https://lccn.loc.gov/2024026730

ISBN: 978-1-032-69291-3 (hbk)
ISBN: 978-1-032-69283-8 (pbk)
ISBN: 978-1-032-69294-4 (ebk)

DOI: 10.4324/9781032692944

Typeset in Optima
by Apex CoVantage, LLC

Contents

A note from the series editor

This book is part of a new series from Routledge, which I am thrilled to be editing. I first got the idea for this series when talking with several practitioners about the definitions of terms I used in my own work around loving pedagogy. I realised it would be helpful to have an amplified dictionary that unpicks the terms used and explains what they mean and look like in practice. Then, I thought that if this idea would work well for explaining a loving pedagogy, it might also work well for other topics, and the idea of 'Key Concepts in Early Childhood' was formed.

This particular book, *Wellbeing Explained,* written by Sonia, is the first in the series, which is very fitting, as children's wellbeing needs to underpin everything we do. Sonia begins by exploring why wellbeing is so important and then unpicks terms used when promoting children's wellbeing, including emotional literacy, dysregulation, holistic development, SEMH, and transitions. At the end of the first section, Sonia shares lots of helpful resources and suggestions for further reading. Then, in part two, she explores the rights of the child, the role of the adult, and wellbeing in terms of policy in more detail.

It was a joy to edit this book, and I know you will learn from Sonia's clear explanations and enjoy dipping into the different sections. I hope this book assists you in your vital role of supporting the wellbeing of young children.

Tamsin Grimmer

Acknowledgement

Thank you to the Nurture Outreach Team for being the best team to work with.

Introduction

This book is part of a new series for Routledge, which I am so pleased to contribute to. In this book, I am going to be explaining the key terms that are often used in the field of wellbeing. The field of wellbeing in the early years is an ever-growing area, which is a good thing; however, there seems to be an increasing number of terms, words, and sometimes jargon used which can be baffling. In the first section of this book, I will be listing many of the terms used in this area and giving a quick explanation of what they mean. In the second part of the book, I will be looking in more detail at the ethos of the setting/school and cover themes linked to this, such as the role of the adult, the rights of the child, and writing a wellbeing policy.

My hope is this will be a book you can dip in and out of. If you are a student and need a quick explanation guide, I hope this book will be hugely beneficial. You may be someone who has worked in the early years for a long time, and you need a quick reminder on some of the new terms; my hope is that this book will be useful for you also. Or you may be a parent, you have heard lots about wellbeing, and you would like some ideas on how to support your child; I hope you will find some useful ideas and suggestions here.

How to use this book

This is one of those books that you can flip through, find a subject you need to read up on, and then take a few minutes to read that section, for example, emotional regulation. Or you might be looking for a bit more information about how to write a wellbeing policy (you will find this in the second part); this will take a bit longer to read, but it is readable with a cup of tea/coffee over a break. Or you might decide to read this book cover to cover, and that will work, too.

Why is wellbeing important?

Wellbeing is a term which sometimes we link with celebrities, pampering, and fads. This is not what wellbeing is about – it is not a luxury, it is not an add-on, and it is not a 'when I have money' thing.

I think to start this book, it might be helpful to define the term wellbeing. There are many different terms out there, but one I have created over the years is:

Feeling loved
Feeling safe
Feeling I belong
Loving my self
Feeling good about who I am
Being able to cope with life's difficulties.

Hopefully, you will be able to look at those words and recognise them for yourself and for the children you work with. But I know there will be others who read those words and think, 'No that is not how I am feeling right now . . .' If that is you, please be kind and gentle to yourself as you read this, and please find some support. Throughout the book, there are many links to organisations and places for help. After this introduction, I have a small section of key places to look if you need some additional support now.

Thankfully, wellbeing is now recognised as a skill, and there are tools we need to learn to embed into our lives to enable us to have good wellbeing; it is not something we can take for granted or think will just happen. Many workplaces now talk about wellbeing and recognise the importance of supporting staff's wellbeing. We know that if staff have a high wellbeing, then stress levels will be lower, staff sickness will be lower, and the workplace will be more effective. Within early years and education, we know that as staff, we need to be in a good place ourselves to be able to support the children's wellbeing. A common phrase we hear is the one that we need to put on our own oxygen mask before we put on our neighbours; we need to address our wellbeing needs first, and then we are equipped to support the children and others around us. Throughout this book, you will find many links to big organisations such as the NHS, the Government, and many charities who, over the last few years, have been offering suggestions and ideas around wellbeing practices. Hopefully, this will confirm to you that wellbeing is not a fad for celebrities!

Wellbeing for all

This book will offer ideas on how we can support adult wellbeing and children's wellbeing. In the definition section, I will be sharing a mix of practitioner ideas and case examples. My intention is to ground the whole book in practice; both practice I am regularly involved in and practice I have observed with others. I am a firm believer that we all need to create a wellbeing toolkit for both ourselves and the children we work with. In your toolkit, there will be tools and strategies to support your wellbeing; we will all have different toolkits, and that is ok. My hope is this book will offer you some ideas that you can put into your toolkit. Just to give you an idea, the following includes a few examples of what is in my wellbeing toolkit for myself and for the children I work with:

My wellbeing toolkit

- Coffee first thing in the morning
- Chamomile tea throughout the day
- Swimming costume (both for pool and wild swimming)
- My garden
- Connection to friends and family
- Books
- Creating something

Children's wellbeing toolkit

- Play dough/clay
- Scripts (I explain these later in the book)
- Hand cream
- Bubbles
- Outdoor space
- Books

Mental health

We all have mental health, and sometimes our mental health is in a good place, and sometimes it is not, just like our physical health. We know we need to look after our physical health by eating well, getting enough sleep, and exercising, and all these massively benefit our mental health too. We now know that mental and physical health are closely linked. I am not a mental health specialist, and this is not a mental health book. I think it is so important that we recognise and name when our mental health is low and that we seek out help and support. This book is not looking to offer specialist guidance around mental health for you or your children. However, I do believe looking after wellbeing is part of looking after our mental and physical health and that of the children we support.

Who am I?

And finally, before we start the book, I thought I should introduce myself. I am a 51-year-old white woman living in Somerset. I live in a village with my husband, who is an artist, and I have two daughters who are 24 and 26. I have worked with children since the age of 16. For the last ten years, I have worked for a small organisation called Brighter Futures, part of Threeways School. Our team supports children with social, emotional, and mental health needs across Bath and North East Somerset. My main role is supporting children in reception classes and nurseries. The children we work with all have low wellbeing. Our role is unique as it enables us to work with the child and the staff, who work with them all year. I love my job; it is a unique and wonderful role within an incredibly experienced team. Supporting the wellbeing of the staff and children is at the centre of all we do, but that is only possible because looking after our own wellbeing underpins all our work. There are a few main ways I support my wellbeing, but the main one for me is cold water swimming. I swim in a pool five mornings a week, but my love and my greatest stress release is cold water swimming. It is the most joyful and enriching experience I know. Alongside my work in schools, I deliver training around children's Social Emotional, and Mental Health (SEMH) and wellbeing, and I also write books. This is my eleventh book.

Layout of the book

In the first part of this book, you will find an alphabetical list of terms. Each term is explained in a couple of paragraphs, and some of them have an example from practice or a practitioner's view with them. There is a list of the terms I am exploring at the top of the section. In between parts one and two, I have added a further links section with suggestions of books and websites linked to each term. In the second part of the book, I explore in a bit more detail key areas of this subject and how we embed wellbeing in our practice, offering guidance and thoughts. At the end of the book, you can find any academic references referred to. They are linked to the text throughout the book using superscript numbers.

I am using the term 'settings' very broadly in this book to encompass childminders, schools, and private, voluntary, and independent settings. In a similar vein, the term 'practitioner' includes all adults who work alongside children regardless of their level of qualification or experience. I am using the term 'parents' to not only include birth-parents, but also any main carers of a child, for example, grandparents, foster carers, or step-parents. Children are referred to using a pseudonym, and wherever possible, children have also been consulted about the use of any case study material or photographs. I have also tried to consider the representation of backgrounds, cultural heritage, settings, and gender to try and ensure this book shares the perspective of others.

I hope you find this book useful.
Key places for support:

NHS – https://www.nhs.uk/mental-health/
Mind – https://www.mind.org.uk/
Young Minds – https://www.youngminds.org.uk/
Anna Freud – https://www.annafreud.org/

Explaining terms

In this section, I will explain different wellbeing terms. These are the terms I will be exploring:

Anxiety	Nature deficit disorder
ACEs	Nurture
Attachment needs	Outdoors
Creativity/imagination	SEMH
Depression	Self-compassion
Dysregulation	Self-harm
Early intervention	Self-esteem
Emotional regulation	Selective mutism
Emotional literacy	Self-regulation
Enabling environment	Spiritual wellbeing
Fight/flight/freeze/fawn	Stress
Holistic development	SSTEW scale
Listening to children	Thrive
Loving pedagogy	Transitions
Leuven scale	Wellbeing
Joyfulness	Window of tolerance
Mental health first aid	

Anxiety

Anxiety is a term we often associate with adults, but over the last few years, we have increasingly heard it in relation to children, including young children. On the NHS website[1], anxiety is described as a feeling of unease, such as worry or fear, that can be mild or severe. It is not unusual to feel anxious at certain times, for example, at the start of an exam or interview or starting a new job. Some people experience anxiety a lot of the time; they may feel anxious at everything new they try or when meeting new people, they may feel anxious every Monday morning or Sunday evening at the thought of the new week, and they may feel anxious leaving their house. Anxiety sometimes presents itself by feeling sick or having pains in your tummy; some people get headaches. Anxiety can affect sleep, causing people to find it hard to sleep or wake. Some people feel their heart racing, or their breathing gets shallower; others experience pins and needles. For some people, anxiety causes panic attacks. The NHS website[2] has a helpful section offering tips on how to manage anxiety. If you, a colleague, or parents/carers you are working with are finding anxiety is impacting everyday life, I would encourage you to speak to a GP.

A PRACTITIONER'S VIEW

As I am writing this section of the book, it is the summer of 2023, and I have just finished with my latest cohort of children in reception class. I described this school year as an anxious year; many of the children I worked with were highly anxious, and some of their parents were anxious, too. Some ways we saw the anxiety in the children were through them being very fearful of trying something new; they would often stand on the side and watch,

DOI: 10.4324/9781032692944-3

bite their lips, or nibble their fingers. When asked if they would like to join in, they would shake their heads, often not speaking. Some children would also hide. Parents were often commenting that the children were finding it hard to sleep. One little boy needed to talk through his day when he got home in lots of detail and was unable to relax until he had spoken through the whole day. Another child was unable to eat with other children; even by the end of the school year, she was still unable to eat food with others. Other children found the toilets very frightening, and it was several weeks until they were able to use the school toilets. Many children would tell parents on a Sunday night that they felt poorly and wouldn't be able to go to school the next day.

So, how can we help an anxious child? My main tip is to go slowly; don't rush things. It is ok to name how they are feeling; a useful phrase can be 'I wonder if you are feeling a bit anxious about going back to school today' or 'I wonder if you are feeling a bit anxious about joining in with that game.' Reassure them that you are there for them. Preparing children can be very helpful; using visual timetables at the start but also throughout the day can help a child who is anxious. Also, using social stories can be a brilliant way to help prepare a child for something. You can write your own or download one. Social stories are traditionally used with children who have autism; however, I have found that it is a useful tool for lots of children, whether they have a diagnosis of autism or not. A useful description of social stories can be found on Sheffield Children's NHS page[3]. I have written social stories about using the toilet, eating in the dining hall, going to forest school, changing for PE, and going on a school trip; the aim is to explain something in a visual, short, and simple way. If you are concerned about a child being highly anxious, talk to the parents about what they are seeing at home; have a conversation with the health visitor and maybe suggest the parents see their GP.

Using the toilet at school social story example:

1. It is ok to use the toilets at school. They might look and sound different from the toilet at home, but they are okay.
2. It is important we use the toilet when we need it. If we don't, it can make us feel uncomfortable and maybe poorly.

3. We can shut the door, which is safe, then we can open it again when we have finished on the toilet.
4. When we have been to the toilet, we always wash our hands with soap and water. This washes away the germs and helps us to stay safe and well.
5. Then, we dry our hands with one paper towel.

ACEs

ACEs stands for adverse childhood experiences. The initial thinking around ACEs came from Dr. Vincent Felitti[4], who was working in San Diego in preventive medicine. He was curious about why many of his patients were dropping out of his weight loss plans. Through questioning his patients, he discovered a common thread that he would later describe as adverse childhood experiences. These are significant negative experiences people have experienced in childhood. Along with other colleagues, he devised a ten-part questionnaire to find out if patients had lived through any of these in their childhood. The list of ten areas are:

1. Emotional abuse
2. Physical abuse
3. Verbal abuse
4. Sexual abuse
5. Neglect
6. Substance abuse in the house
7. Mental illness in the household
8. Domestic violence
9. Divorce or parental separation
10. Criminal behaviour in the household

Through this study, they found that if you have experienced several ACEs in childhood, there is a higher chance this could have a negative impact on your physical and mental health later in life.

Dr. Nadine Harris, a leading Paediatrician, took this work forward and wrote a book in 2018 called *The Deepest Well: Healing the Long-term Effects of Childhood Adversity*[5]. Her work has helped us to understand the impact trauma can have on a child and the way this can

     DOI: 10.4324/9781032692944-4

impact their adulthood, but importantly, she has also led the way in exploring how we can alleviate the impact of ACEs.

If you would like to learn about ACEs, I would recommend watching a mini film made by the Welsh public health team on ACEs[6]. I also recommend reading Nadine Harris's book. I also want to make clear that the original questionnaire was made by health professionals for health professionals; the aim was not for other agencies, such as education, to use them with families.

A PRACTITIONER'S VIEW

How useful is it to understand ACEs? This has been a question that we have discussed and reflected on a lot in our team. I believe it is vital to have an understanding of the lives and experiences of the children we work with. For example, when the school team and I know that a child we are supporting has been living in or still lives in a household with domestic violence or drug misuse, this helps us to have a greater understanding if the child is anxious, hyper-vigilant, or violent. With this information, we can better offer the child a place of safety, love, and understanding without judgment. However, we are also aware that every child and person is different. Because individuals have experienced ACEs, this does not mean they are absolutely destined to have serious lifelong conditions as a result of their ACEs. We need to be careful as practitioners that we hold the information in a way that helps us with the child and family but does not cause us to make judgments or presumptions.

Attachment needs

From birth, we all form bonds or attachments to the main people who are around us; these bonds are usually with parents/carers. This helps us to feel safe and protected. In the early years, we regularly use the term 'secure attachment.' This describes a child who feels safe and secure with their main caregiver; they turn to them when they need love, safety, and security, and their needs are met when they seek them.

There are other terms that are used within attachment:

Avoidant attachment: This is when a child's needs have not been met, e.g., a child who was crying for food or because they were wet, and the parent/carer did not respond to them. These children can get to the point where they don't recognise their own needs and don't seek help if they are hurt, upset, or frightened. You may see this with children who don't come to the adults for comfort or when they have hurt themselves.

Ambivalent attachment: This is when a child does not know if their needs will be met. In their experience, sometimes their parent/carer meets their needs, but sometimes they do not. Sometimes, these children don't know who they can trust. You may see this with children who are cautious around the staff who work with them; they find it hard to talk to and trust the adults around them.

Disorganised attachment: This is where a child feels scared of their parents/carer. Their experience is that parents/carers are not safe; they are frightening, and their behaviour can be harmful and neglectful. Often, these children feel the world and everyone around them are frightening. You may see this with children who flinch when adults come near them or hide or move away from adults.

 DOI: 10.4324/9781032692944-5

For more information, the Anna Freud website[7] has a basic leaflet about how we can support a child's attachment. If this is an area you would like to explore further, I recommend looking at Dan Siegel's books with Dr. Tina Payne Bryson[8]; they are aimed at parents but useful for all of us. It is important to remember it is not our place to diagnose an attachment difficulty, but we can raise questions, be curious, and raise concerns with the Special Educational Needs Coordinator (SENCO), the Area SENCO (usually employed by the local authority), and other professionals working with the family such as health visitors and social workers.

Creativity/imagination

Just for a moment, think about what you do that is creative and imaginative in your life. The COVID-19 lockdowns were a time when many people realised how important creativity is for our well-being, with many people taking up knitting, learning an instrument, baking, and many other creative endeavours. Creativity can be a way of helping us to let go of stresses and concerns; it can be a way in which we can become focused on something completely different from our everyday lives and work. I have realised that the more stressed and busy I am, the more I create. In term 6, just before the end of the last school year, I was creating and making far more than I had done all year. I discovered the joy of printing and started to print leaf prints on different-sized paper, material, and bags. I was also baking a lot. These creative outputs were a massive stress relief for me as the term was becoming busier and more complicated, and my brain felt like it was fit to burst. They didn't take lots of time, and I am fortunate that my children are now grown up, so I have more time to spare, but they did act as a huge release for me from my workdays.

Creativity with children is more than just offering a few pens, pencils, and paper; it is about how we open up the exciting, diverse, and colourful world of creativity, enabling children to create and experiment with colours, make sculptures, discover felting and printing, sing and dance, create puppet shows and mini-plays, experiment with words, and share stories. Creativity is a fantastic way to help children express themselves and explore their emotions and feelings. In early years, we have a rich history of offering creative practices with children, but sadly, this is happening less further through education, with many schools finding they have less time to offer creative

DOI: 10.4324/9781032692944-6

opportunities. For this reason, I believe it is even more important to offer a wide range of creative opportunities in early years and share with children different examples of creative practices. You might like to invite in a grandparent or parent who knits, plays an instrument, or draws to share this with the children.

Figure 1.1

CASE EXAMPLE

Using clay: In the summer of 2020, I was involved in running a two-week play scheme for primary-aged children who were identified as having high social, emotional, and mental health needs and were particularly isolated through the lockdowns. One of the continuous provisions in the play scheme was clay, and we had an artist working with us who specialised in using clay. The children didn't have to use clay, but many chose to, and many of them had not used clay before. I discovered one of the wonderful aspects of using clay is how therapeutic and calming it can be, or for some, how therapeutic and releasing it can be. Because the clay was available every day throughout the session, many children started something and then would come back to their work to add to it, adapt it, and extend it. This reminded me of the practice I have seen in Reggio Emilia pre-schools. Reggio Emilia[9] is well known for its creative practice with early years children; it is a small northern town in Italy where the preschools are recognised for their unique approach; see links at the end for further information. Through using the clay, some children were creating objects such as bowls, animals, and pots; others were creating mini worlds and stories to go with their world. One girl made a small forest with animals and people to go in her forest and created a story around this. When we asked the children at the end of the play scheme what they enjoyed about the two weeks, many mentioned how much they loved using clay. Since the play scheme, I have used clay in my nurture sessions with the four-year-olds I support. I have found it to be such a wonderful open-ended material to use with children; some children find it nurturing and calming, and other children have loved pounding it and using it to let out their strong emotions.

For more information on how important creativity is for children's wellbeing, you may like to look at my book[10], *Creativity and Wellbeing in the Early Years*.

Depression

The NHS website[11] describes depression as a low mood that can last a long time or keep returning, affecting your everyday life. The Mind website[12] describes how some people with milder depression may have a low mood but are still able to carry on with their daily life, but they may find that everyday accomplishments feel harder. Some people with more severe depression may find everyday life events too hard to manage; some people with severe depression experience suicidal thoughts.

There are several different forms of depression, some of which you may have heard of; SAD (Seasonal Affective Disorder) is a depression that occurs in certain seasons of the year, Postnatal depression is depression that occurs in the first year after giving birth, and it can affect both partners. As a workplace, it is important that we are aware of how to support colleagues who are struggling with their mental health. Later in this chapter, I have a section on mental health first aid which links to this. It is also important to keep in mind the parents we work with who may also be experiencing depression.

Depression doesn't just exist in adults; it can occur in children, too. The way we sometimes see it in children includes:

- Sadness, not just occasionally but often
- Struggling to sleep
- Anxiety/worry
- Feeling tired a lot of the time
- Being grumpy
- Finding it hard to concentrate
- Less interested in life/friends

DOI: 10.4324/9781032692944-7

If you think a child is showing signs of depression, talk to their parents, have a conversation with the health visitor, and suggest the parents speak to the GP. The NHS website[13] has some useful information on depression in children.

A PRACTITIONER'S VIEW

Many children will live in a family where a member of the family is experiencing a mental illness, and as educators, we don't always know this information. This will have an impact on the child, and it does change the dynamics in the family. I am writing this from personal experience; I grew up with a mum who has Bipolar. I think it is helpful as educators to be aware of this information so that we can offer the child additional support. I work with many children where mental illness is part of their family life; sometimes, this leads to the child feeling worried, a bit tearful, and sometimes angry. One way we can support children and families is by helping them to understand through stories about mental illness. In the further reading section, I have suggested a few books that might be helpful for children, including one about depression in adults. As well as supporting the child with this, don't be afraid to ask parents how they are, enquire after their health, and explain how you are trying to support the child.

Dysregulation

This is a word often used to describe when a child is very upset, feels overwhelmed, and is unable to regulate their emotions. This is not about the child choosing to be dysregulated; it is out of their control. Different things can trigger dysregulation, and it will be different for every child; sometimes, this is affected by them being tired, overwhelmed, overly stimulated, hungry, frightened, or anxious. Dysregulation is the opposite of self-regulation. I firmly believe that all behaviour from children is a form of communication, and our role as adults is to be able to understand what the child is telling us. Tamsin Grimmer[14], in her book *Supporting behaviour and emotions in the early years*, has a phrase called 'behaviour detective.' I love this phrase, and it is one I have used many times; she calls on us to become behaviour detectives to help us understand what is underpinning the child's behaviour and what it is they are communicating to us. I think this is also a valuable insight we can share with parents. So many times, I have heard children say the child is choosing to be difficult or choosing to defy the parent; we need to gently explain and help parents to understand this is not about choice; the child is telling us how unhappy they are, our job is to try and find out what is making them unhappy.

A PRACTITIONER'S VIEW

Many of the children I support through my nurture role regularly become dysregulated. For some children, this looks like a full-blown tantrum, sometimes screaming and hitting; for other children, this looks like hiding or freezing. When a child is dysregulated, they are totally overwhelmed; their wellbeing is

DOI: 10.4324/9781032692944-8

extremely low, and they are often feeling scared. When a child is dysregulated, they often cannot hear the adult's voice or make sense of any words being said; however, sometimes they can hear a gentle sing-song voice. When a child is dysregulated, they need adults who are calm and loving, who are able to be alongside them, and who are there to help them feel calmer and safer. You will often find me sitting alongside a child who is dysregulated, sometimes humming or gently singing, sometimes blowing bubbles. Then, when the child is able to cope with having an adult near them, I will ask them if they need holding or have their arm stroked or if they are ready to join me in blowing bubbles. It is important that all adults understand that children need love, calmness, and a regulated adult alongside them when they are dysregulated; an adult shouting at them will not help the situation. The writer Mona Delahooke[15,16] has excellent books for educators and parents on how we can support children's behaviour; links at the end of the chapter.

Early intervention

This is a term you may have heard; it is about recognising that the sooner we can support a child and their family when they are beginning to struggle, the potentially better outcome for the child and family. Early Intervention Foundation[17] has a short video that simply explains this term and how it works in the UK. Unfortunately, early intervention has become quite politicised in the UK. When Labour was in government, they introduced the Sure Start system, which offered early support to a large number of families with young children. This has slowly disappeared with many cutbacks. Early intervention is a term that we hear again; there are local authority teams and children's charities that still offer some support, home visits, schoolwork, and occasionally groups for vulnerable families to access. It is recognised that if we can offer help and support early on when a family is finding it hard, this will hopefully minimise the chances of them later needing more expensive support through the criminal justice system, social services, and longer-term health services. The term for this early intervention is called early help, and the aim is to improve outcomes for children and prevent escalation of difficulties.

How do we help families access early support? As early years practitioners, we can help to signpost families we are concerned about. If you have a family that you feel is struggling with everyday life and caring for their children, this might be due to financial worries, poor health, death and bereavement, or other reasons. Speak to your manager about your concerns, then have a conversation with the health visitor or maybe make a referral to the local early help team in your area. An early help referral is for a child/family where you have concerns, but it is not at the level of a child protection referral. Knowing what level of support a child/family needs can sometimes be confusing. Rachel Buckler[18] has written an excellent book on safeguarding; in this book, she has a really useful section on understanding levels of needs. It is worth each early years setting having a copy of her book to refer to.

DOI: 10.4324/9781032692944-9

Emotional regulation

As I mentioned previously, emotional regulation is the opposite of dysregulation. I love this description of emotional regulation on Mona Delahook's website[19]:

> Emotional regulation is the springboard of mental health. Assisting children in developing this capacity helps them develop psychological resilience that serves them for years to come.

Assisting children in developing their emotional regulation is a key role for all of us daily. The main way we do this is by noticing children's emotional needs and then appropriately responding to them. Ideally, this needs to happen before birth, with parents speaking to the baby in the womb, acknowledging them, and responding gently and lovingly to their movements. When the baby arrives, they need their carers to respond to their needs and use emotionally attuned language to let the baby know their needs are seen, heard, and responded to. For example, *"Oh, I can hear you crying; I wonder if you need changing. Let me see if you do.'* This is language we then continue to use as the child grows and develops. Young children need emotionally regulated adults to help them with their emotional regulation.

It is important that we recognise how we are feeling and responding to situations. There will be times when we feel tired, stressed, or frustrated, which can make it hard to support a child. Recognising our own feelings first is vital before we are able to step in to support the child. Sometimes, we need to stop, take a few deep breaths, speak kindly to ourselves first, and then step in to support the child. Also, knowing what helps us to stay emotionally regulated is important. For me, having enough sleep and eating properly during the day is vital. If I am tired and hungry, that does not help me to be emotionally regulated.

DOI: 10.4324/9781032692944-10

Emotional literacy

Emotional literacy is about having the words to describe how you feel; another term for this is emotional vocabulary. Just for a moment, sit and think about how many different emotion words you can name. Brené Brown's latest book, *Atlas of the Heart*[20], explores and names 87 different emotions. Over the years, I have become pretty good at naming and recognising emotions, but 87 is a lot more than I managed to name! Brené Brown is a research professor at the University of Houston, as well as a writer. As part of this role, she collated surveys from over seven thousand students who attended some of her training; they were asked to list all the emotions they could recognise and name. The average number of emotions named was three: happy, sad, and angry. In her book, she suggests that 'language is our portal to meaning-making, connection, healing, and learning' (p. 21).

I believe that as early years practitioners, it is vital we share a wide emotional vocabulary with children. I love it when I see a three-year-old in the street shouting at their parent and saying, '*I am angry.*' This might sound strange, but I take joy in the fact that the child can name how they feel. What we also need is for children to gain a really rich and wide emotional vocabulary as they grow older. But recognising and naming their feeling is a fantastic start. In addition to helping children to have an emotional language, we also need to help them understand that emotions are neither positive nor negative; they just are what they are. Too often, we can pin negative views onto emotions, and this is not helpful for anyone. We also importantly need to help children recognise what their needs are and what it is that is triggering their emotional reaction. Are they feeling angry, or is something else going on? In the previous example, is the child angry, or are they tired of walking and feeling hungry? A way we can react to this is by acknowledging the child in the moment and helping them to wonder what is going on in

DOI: 10.4324/9781032692944-11   **25**

their body, for example: '*I can hear you saying you are really angry; I wonder if your legs are tired, and I wonder if you're feeling hungry? When I feel like that, I often feel cross. Would you like something to eat to help you get home?*'

A PRACTITIONER'S VIEWPOINT

So, how can we help children develop an emotional vocabulary? As I mentioned in the emotional regulation section, it is about recognising and naming children's emotions from the moment they are born. In my role as a nurture worker, the teams I work with and I use scripts a lot. The script is something we all use and encourage parents to use, too. An example of this could be: '*Lucy, I am wondering if you are feeling frustrated because Polly did not listen to you. It's ok to feel frustrated, but it's not ok to shout at her.*' Or '*It's ok Bas; I am here. You seem a bit cross. I am wondering if you are feeling hungry. Here, let me find you some food.*' By using these scripts, we are using curiosity around how the child is feeling and offering an emotional language for what they might be experiencing. We are not telling them what they are feeling, but we are helping them to think about what they are experiencing. We need to ensure that we are using an emotional vocabulary throughout the day, not just at those times when a child may be finding something hard. We can also use games, tools, and books to help us embed emotional literacy in our practice.

Many of us, myself included, have been using lots of emotion resources to help children understand their emotions, and I have recently been reading and listening to some thoughts that query this. Questions have been raised about how we use emotion resources by Lisa Feldman Barrett[21] through her neuroscience research. Her concern is around the limitation we see with a lot of these resources, particularly when we have just six or maybe eight faces to describe emotions. Lisa argues that this way of understanding and teaching emotions is based on the assumption that there is an emotion centre in the brain and that we have a blueprint of emotions, but Lisa and her colleagues dispute this idea. Her proposal is that we need to teach children about what is going on in their bodies and how this makes us feel. If we only know the words happy, angry, and sad, then we are hugely constricted in how we understand what is going on for us. Her difficulty around faces/emojis to explain emotions is that the same facial expression can be used in different emotions; for example, a face that looks like someone is screaming could be a scream of disgust, fear, joy, excitement, or anticipation. Also, emotions can show themselves in different ways; for example, when we are feeling happy, we might smile, laugh, or even sometimes cry; therefore, the picture of a smiling face is too simplistic. So the question is, what does this mean for our work with children? This is something I have been thinking a lot about recently. My current feeling is that I am going to continue to use some of my emotion resources as a tool, but not as a definitive. I like to think I have been doing this anyway, but I will be doing it with more intention, that is, using more words, explaining more, and wondering more. Instead of just saying I am wondering if you're feeling angry, an alternative could be saying, *'I can see your fists are clenched and your face is red. I am wondering if you're angry because Lucy hit you, or maybe you're feeling hurt or maybe afraid of her, but I can see they are big feelings you have.'* Throughout this book, I have suggested many stories we can use with children to help them understand the world around them and the feelings they might be experiencing. I still think books are so beneficial for helping us support children's emotional understanding, and we can build on the language used in the books. Instead of just reading the words written down, we can use these to expand and extend the children's vocabulary by adding in other thoughts; for example, when I used a book this week and it said the character was happy, I wondered if she was feeling excited because she was seeing her granny, we then talked about when they have felt excited and how it felt in their body.

Enabling environment

The environment in which we spend our time, such as a nursery room, classroom, or home, can have a significant impact on our wellbeing. Take a moment to think about environments where you feel calm. How do they look, and how do they feel? Now, consider an environment that makes you feel agitated, uneasy, or perhaps unsafe. Of course, everyone is different, and what helps one person feel calm can agitate others.

There are things we can do in an environment to help both children and staff feel welcome and safe. For children with additional sensory needs, as well as those with social, emotional, and mental health needs, the environment can significantly impact their wellbeing. Environments that are loud and cluttered with items hanging from the ceiling and lots of colour everywhere can act as overly sensory stimulation and become distressing for some children and adults. I recommend regularly doing a mini-check of your environment, looking around the space from a child's view, and possibly getting on your knees to see it from their height. If it looks cluttered, address this. Elizabeth Jarman[22] wrote a book with many ideas about creating an enabling environment that supports children's communication and wellbeing. She suggests using materials on walls and as hangings to help make the space quieter, thinking about the resources in your space, and creating spaces like cozy corners.

In many Scandinavian early years settings, there is a regular practice of bringing the outside into the setting. We know that being outside in nature is beneficial for everyone's wellbeing, and bringing nature inside can also support wellbeing. Throughout spring and summer, I bring flowers from my garden into my house; they make me smile and give me a mini boost to my wellbeing.

 DOI: 10.4324/9781032692944-12

CASE EXAMPLE

In my area, there is a village preschool based in a village hall with limited space. During a recent visit, I noticed how they had turned one side of the hall into a sitting room space. It featured a small child-sized sofa, a rug on the floor, a bookcase with a lamp, larger floor cushions, framed art posters on the wall, a mirror, flowers in a vase on the windowsill, and material hanging down from the ceiling. This part of the preschool space felt inviting, warm, and welcoming. Next to it was a pretend kitchen area with real crockery, cutlery, kitchen equipment, and a small table with chairs. Reading about it may sound like a provision you see in every nursery, but this felt different. It really felt like a home, with items found in a home, not a children's plastic version of a home. When I asked the staff about it, they told me they had added to and adapted it over time, with the intention of making it feel like home, and the children responded well to this. Sometimes, if children were sad, they would take themselves to this space as they found it comforting.

Fight/flight/freeze/fawn

This term is used to describe how our bodies sometimes respond to threats or danger. Our bodies are amazing at trying to protect us; if we were in a field with cows charging towards us, we would probably immediately start to run very fast. The brain reacts quickly and sends messages to other parts of our body to react; it does this instinctively. How it feels in our body is that, often, our hearts will start racing; we might feel clammy or sweaty; we feel super alert. The difficulty with this response is that sometimes our brains perceive a threat when there isn't one and still jump into this response.

I am going to briefly describe each of the descriptors and how we might see this in children:

Fight: In many ways, this is obvious, and we can probably all think of fight situations we have seen or heard of. You may see it in a child when they become dysregulated, hitting and kicking out at anyone around them.

Flight: This is when someone flees or runs away from a situation. If a child feels scared, they may run and run; I have seen children run across large playgrounds and scale high fences and then run along a road. Once this response kicks in, they can be very fast.

Freeze: This can be harder to spot; sometimes, it is obvious – the child stops and does not respond. However, sometimes, if it is a busy space with lots of noise and activity, it can be hard to spot. I have worked with several children who had freeze responses; as staff, we needed to be tuned into how this looked for the child.

Fawn: This is about being submissive, not feeling able to fight/argue/ disagree; it is thought to come from a place of hoping that if you

DOI: 10.4324/9781032692944-13

agree to do something, you are in less danger. You might see this in a child who always seems to agree with everything and doesn't stand up for themselves.

If you would like to learn about this area and how our brains respond (the brain science behind it is fascinating), I highly recommend Debbie Garvey's *Little Brains Matter* book (2023)[23].

Holistic development

We use the term holistic development to describe looking at the whole of the child, recognising that each part of a child's development is important, and every child is different. Settings and practitioners who use a holistic development approach will be looking at the child's physical, emotional, social, intellectual, spiritual, and cultural development, recognising these as all important, and no one aspect is more important than another. Looking at each child in this way enables us to see and celebrate every individual child rather than trying to place them within a narrow framework. Using a holistic development approach works for every child and family; it helps us to capture and support each individual child's needs. Practitioners who embed this approach use observations as a key part of understanding and supporting every child. The observations help practitioners understand children's interests; they can use these to plan and support this. If you would like to understand this more, I would suggest looking at an article on the Parenta website[24] and also looking at the *Birth to Five Matters* website[25]. The *Birth to Five Matters* website offers guidance on how to implement the early years foundation stage with a holistic approach. Using a holistic approach benefits everyone and is especially helpful when we are working with children with additional needs, as it helps us to view what they can do rather than focus on what they can't do. Kerry Payne's book, *Supporting the Wellbeing of Children with SEND*[26], explores this in more detail. When we are thinking about holistic development, we need to remember to think about the family and the culture that the child is part of, to be curious, find out, and inquire; this forms an important part of our anti-racist practice. Valerie Daniel[27] explores this more in her new book, offering many ideas and suggestions on how we can embed anti-racist practices.

DOI: 10.4324/9781032692944-14

Listening to children

Being listened to is essential for all of us. When we are not listened to, we can feel disempowered, neglected, unloved. Listening to children is essential in our daily practice; we need to listen to the child every day in small moments, such as when a child is hungry, thirsty, tired, too hot, or wanting to tell us something important to them. We also need to listen to them in the big moments, such as when they are telling us something has happened to them. Listening to the child is more than just hearing the words they are using; it is about how we watch, notice, observe their behaviour, and recognise changes in their body language. We can listen to the child by following their interests, such as knowing what they like and dislike. For example, putting out the dinosaurs every day because you know Jamel loves dinosaurs and settles when he plays with these first. But also listening to the child in the bigger areas and noticing when things change for them. Maybe they are coming in dirtier; maybe they are eating a lot more during the day; maybe they have more bruises on their legs. Truly listening to the child is a powerful act. Recognising that listening is more than words and embedding this into our practice is so essential for a child's wellbeing. If you look back over many case reviews of children who have died, tragically, the repeated phrase we see is the child was not listened to.

A PRACTITIONER'S VIEW

Before my job as a nurture consultant, I led a team embedding listening to children's practice across the local authority where I worked. I worked with staff to involve children from ages 2–18 in staff recruitment, planning parks, planning in Sure Start centres

DOI: 10.4324/9781032692944-15

and schools, and involving children in giving feedback to hospital staff and social services. In that time, the key component I learned was to take a step back for a moment and view the world through the child's eyes; using the mosaic approach by Clarke and Moss[28] really helped this. Part of the mosaic approach is getting children to take photos of what matters to them. These were powerful tools to help the local authority make changes. The other powerful tool was observing, watching, and listening to the whole of the child, not just their words, to get a sense of what was important to them. These are essential tools I have taken with me into my current role as a nurture consultant; observation is vital and underpins all that I do, stepping back and watching, noticing, often the small things such as a change in body posture, facial expression can inform me of so much. Also, I still use photography with the children, and every year in term 6, they take photos of what they enjoy in school, and we use this as part of their transition documents to inform their new teachers about them. For more information on the many ways we can listen to children in our work, you may like to look at one of my books, *Listening to Young Children in Early Years Setting*[29].

Loving pedagogy

The term loving pedagogy is inspired by the work of Dr. Jools Page[30], who developed a term called professional love (2011). Dr. Page was involved in a research project with a research team and a small number of nurseries in the South East of England. The project was called Professional Love in Early Years Settings[31]. Tamsin Grimmer was inspired by this work and research; she went on to develop further writing and training in this area. Tamsin suggests we need to reclaim the word love and loving pedagogy for our work. In her book *Developing a Loving Pedagogy in Early Years*[32], Tamsin suggests that love is not just a feeling or an emotion but also a deliberate act, an intention, an action. Her book explores how we embed a loving pedagogy within all our practices with children. Tamsin's new book *Loving Pedagogy Explained*[33], which is another book in this series, further unpicks this approach and is well worth dipping into.

For a moment, think about how you show the children in your setting that you love them.

CASE EXAMPLE

The children I work with in my nurture role have all been allocated some money by the local authority to have additional support in the classroom; this is usually through having a teaching assistant supporting them for some of the time. When I meet a new teaching assistant, I often explain to them that their primary role is to love the child; sometimes, this can come as a bit of a surprise. One little boy I was supporting was finding school a huge challenge; he was often overwhelmed, frightened, and confused.

He showed this by regularly becoming extremely dysregulated, sometimes hiding and often hitting out. His teaching assistant was often angry about this behaviour; she was convinced he deliberately wanted to be difficult and that he was choosing to behave in this way. We spent a lot of time together talking about the little boy's story, his experience of life, how he saw the world, and why this might be his view. I spent a lot of time modelling another approach for her, one coming from a place of love, acceptance, and kindness. With the little boy, I had really clear boundaries and was clear about no hitting, but I also showed playfulness, love, kindness, and gentleness. Over time, the teaching assistant began to see and understand why the little boy was so frightened and how his behaviour was his way of telling us it was all too much. It was an incredibly intense year for many sad reasons, but the relationship between the boy and his teaching assistant became one of the most beautiful relationships I have seen. Basically, in the end, she loved him. She was kind and compassionate, she was playful, she had boundaries, and she was clear about these, but she loved him, and he thrived on this love. By the end of the school year, the boy moved to another school. I occasionally still hear about his progress and occasionally still see his teaching assistant; she still asks after him and says he is one child she will never forget. There is a phrase 'love wins,' and without a doubt, the way she learned to love him made a huge difference to both of them and to me. Love won.

Leuven scale

The Leuven scale is also called the wellbeing and involvement scale. It is a tool that has been created by Ferre Laevers, director of the Research Centre for Experiential Education at the University of Leuven. He has created two simple scales we can use as part of our observations of a child to try and help us understand how involved they are in their play and to help us understand their wellbeing levels. There is a scale for wellbeing and a scale for involvement. In the scales, there are five levels to look at, with a description for each level; these range from extremely low, low, moderate, high, and extremely high. You use the scales as a tool whilst observing the child.

Laever's theory is that high levels of wellbeing and involvement enable children to experience deep levels of learning. Laevers and his team have a descriptor of signs of wellbeing, these are:

- The child has an openness and is able to take on new ideas and changes in the environment and people around them
- The child has flexibility; this means being able to cope with changes and adapt
- The child shows self-confidence and has good self-esteem; they can express themselves and can cope when they can't do something
- The child can be assertive; they are able to speak out for themselves and say what they like, dislike, or don't want
- The child has vitality; they are active, full of life and energy, and keen to try things and have a go
- The child is able to be relaxed and at peace; they can be still, have times of being peaceful and calm

DOI: 10.4324/9781032692944-17

- The child shows enjoyment; they experience joy and delight, and you can see this in the face and body and sounds
- The child is aware of their feelings, wishes, and thoughts and can express these

Leicestershire County Council website[34] has a link to the scales that you can print off and further links to how Pen Green uses these scales. Pen Green is a children's centre with an excellent reputation.

A PRACTITIONER'S VIEW

The Leuven scales have become a vital tool in my work. At the start of each school year, I always spend several weeks observing the children and trying to discover what they like, what works for them, and what they find hard. Using the scales as part of this observation gives me more insight into what I am seeing. I often find it easy to spot the really low level of wellbeing (level 1 on the scale); the child often looks sad, they don't have a sparkle in their eyes, their body sometimes appears limp, and they often have little energy. It's the middle area that can be harder to identify (level 3); these children often appear at first to be joining in and engaging, but they find transitions hard, or they find it challenging when there is a change or another child joins in the play. These are the children that we often do not realise that their wellbeing is low, and sometimes we miss it. I will often use the levels in my observations and discuss these with staff, then get the staff to use them. I also suggest that staff use them with a child who they feel they don't fully understand or are unsure of what is going on for a child. In my experience, they are such a useful tool.

Joyfulness

I want you to take a moment and think about what brings you joy. For me, it is swimming outside in wild places. As I write this, I can immediately bring to mind swimming in the Outer Hebrides in crystal clear turquoise water. It's cold but amazing.

In Brene Brown's book *Atlas of the Heart*[20], she describes joy as a 'sudden, unexpected short lasting, high intensity. It's characterised by a connection with others, or with God, nature, or the universe' (p. 204). She suggests that joy is different from happiness, which is often more stable, longer lasting, and lower in intensity of feelings to joy. Brene also believes that joy is closely linked to gratitude. There is an interview on Woman's Hour[35] where Brene explores how having an active practice of gratitude and being grateful for things in your life invites more joy into your life. I have found this really helpful. On my desktop, I have a joy photo board, which has photos of things that bring me joy. In those moments of engaging in these, I try hard to take a moment and give thanks for them. While outdoor swimming, I usually give thanks inwardly and sometimes out loud for being in the cold water and how it makes me feel.

A PRACTITIONER'S VIEW

Once we know what brings us joy and we practice this with gratitude, we also need to help children be aware of what makes them joyful. We have all seen children in moments of utter, complete joy, that might be while they are playing in a puddle and laughing with delight at their splashes or the joy from reading a familiar story which they love and know so well and laugh

DOI: 10.4324/9781032692944-18

uncontrollably at the story or pictures. In these moments, I wonder how often we notice and tell the child what we have seen, such as, *'Oh Lily I wonder if you are feeling so much joy right now, you are laughing lots and smiling, it is wonderful to see.'* We often comment to children when they are feeling sad or angry, but how often do we also name their emotions of joy and happiness?

There is a saying that the brain is like Velcro for negative experiences and Teflon for positive. In other words, negative experiences naturally stick to the brain, but we need to work on positive experiences sticking to the brain. The way we do that is by recognising and acknowledging the joyful experience, really feeling it and relishing it, and sitting with it for several seconds. By doing this, we help the positive to stick to the brain, and we can later recall it. We can help children do this by noticing, commenting on, and joining in with their moments of joy. We can also help parents and carers recognise when their child is experiencing joy and share that with them. For many of the children I work with, parents hear about the difficult times in the day, and I encourage staff to also share the joyful moments. Sometimes, when we have a child who has many tricky moments in a day, we can lose sight of the joyful times. We all need to hold onto these for both the child's wellbeing and also as an encouragement to the parent/carers and practitioners supporting the child.

Mental health first aid

This is a term which is being used a lot more. We all have mental health, just like we all have physical health. Sometimes, we will have mental ill health, just like sometimes we will have physical ill health. Thankfully, now there is less of a taboo in talking about mental ill health, although I think, in some places, there is still a stigma around it, and some people are afraid to say if their mental health is poor as they are concerned about the repercussions of acknowledging that. An organisation called Mental Health First Aid[36] has developed a training programme to help people recognise, understand, and support people who have mental ill health. The role of the course is not to diagnose but to support people in recognising the warning signs of ill mental health. Many schools now have mental health first aid trained staff, and a rising number of nurseries also have staff trained in this.

We know that early years and education can, at times, be a stressful environment to work in, and adding stresses from our home life can have an impact on our mental health. It is so important that we know the signs and signals to look out for when becoming mentally ill. Kate Moxley is a mental health first aid trainer, and she has written a book, *A Guide to Mental Health for Early Educators*[37], aimed specifically at early years workers, recognising the stresses that we can encounter in the role and the many different things that can generally impact our mental health. Kate offers many ideas about recognising what is going on for us and noticing and paying attention to our mental health. I recommend this book for all early years workplaces.

DOI: 10.4324/9781032692944-19

Nature deficit disorder

Nature deficit disorder is a phrase you may have heard before. It originally came from Richard Louv, who used the term in his book *Last Child in the Woods*[38]. Since then, the phrase has been used to think about how children (and adults) are spending less time outside and don't have a regular connection with nature. There is concern that this is not only a problem for our physical and mental wellbeing but also a problem for our world. If we are not connected to nature, how can we protect the world?

Since 2005, there has been far greater knowledge about the urgent need to protect our world, and there are many excellent ways and examples of how we can engage children in this. Back in 2005, Richard was concerned at how disconnected children were from outside spaces and nature. Through research, he found children were spending more time inside and more time on electric devices. Many are concerned this is only getting worse, particularly since the pandemic. In 2017, Robert Mcfarlane and Jackie Morris made a beautiful book called *The Lost Words*[39], a book naming and picturing words linked to nature that had been taken out of the Oxford children's dictionary. This book became a huge success, with many schools having copies. It has won many awards, and rightly so; it is a beautiful book. Again, it was linked with the idea of children losing their connection to nature. Many of the words in their book are basic nature words such as conker, magpie, dandelion, bluebell, and blackberry. Just for a moment, think about your own connection to nature. When was the last time you were in nature? Maybe in a park or woods, or maybe you are fortunate to have a garden. Now, think about the children you work with. When was the last time they were in nature? Do you encourage the families you work with to engage in nature? Maybe you could have information about free local nature spots in your setting.

DOI: 10.4324/9781032692944-20

CASE EXAMPLE

I spend a lot of time outside with the children I work with, partly because I have noticed how calmer they often are but also because I know it boosts their wellbeing. An activity I regularly do with the children is a nature walk and picture. We each have a plain postcard with double-sided sticky tape on it. We go for a walk in their school area and find things from nature to add to the card. This might be leaves, feathers, petals, or flowers, such as dandelion. We also regularly go out with a magnifying box to look for bugs. I have been doing these activities for years, but in the last few years, I have noticed that many of the children do not have the words to name what they are seeing. I have started to write a list of the words they don't know. On the list, some of the words are dandelion, daisy, buttercup, ladybird, caterpillar, blackberry, worm, woodlouse, and spider. With this in mind, I have become more intentional about naming what we see, not presuming they know, and I always share with the teachers what the children know or don't know. I suggest you give it a go. Even if you don't make a picture, spend time outside with the children you work with and find out what names they have for the nature around them, where you notice gaps, and fill these in for the children. Children of this age love learning new words and names for things, and you never know – you might be supporting a budding botanist (person who studies plants) or entomologist (person who studies insects).

Figure 1.2

Nurture

The Oxford Learners Dictionary[40] definition of nurture is: 'to care for and protect somebody/something while they are growing and developing.' I love the word nurture. The title of my job is nurture consultant for the nurture outreach service; it's the best job title and team name I have worked with. As educators, we all need to be nurturers as part of our role with children. For me, a key part of nurturing a child is supporting, loving, being present, and advocating for the child I am working with. In my role, I work with a small number of children (nine this year), and I support them throughout their reception year. I only see them once a week, but when I see them, my aim is for the children to know I am there for them and that I am thrilled to see them. I welcome them with a huge smile, using words to tell them how pleased I am to see them, a hug if that is what they want, and they have my attention. My aim is for the children to know I love them as they are, and it doesn't matter how big their feelings are or how scary their feelings are; I am there for them. For a moment, I want you to think about how you nurture the children you work with and then think about whether this is a word you regularly use in your work. I feel it is a word we don't use enough; we talk about playing and educating, and we now increasingly talk about love, but I would also like us to embed the word nurturing more, too. I believe that nurturing child is an essential part of boosting and increasing their wellbeing.

CASE EXAMPLE

I realise my role is a very unusual one. I am a peripatetic worker in schools with reception classes, working 1–1 with children with SEMH needs. I currently work in eight schools and two nurseries. I thought I would describe my average day in the first few weeks

DOI: 10.4324/9781032692944-21

of working in my role – if there ever is an average day! In the first few weeks, I observe the child, but once I have started the 1–1 nurture work, I will arrive at a school, greet the teacher/teaching assistant and have a quick catch-up, then find the child. When I see the child, I aim to have a big warm smile, a calm and relaxed body, and words such as 'Hi Freddie, I am so pleased to see you today,' often the child asks what I have with me that day, within a few weeks the children learn that I bring a bag with something for us to share and play with. We usually go and find a quiet spot where we can play; sometimes, we chat as we go, or sometimes, we just walk in silence; I will take the child's lead on this. We then explore what is in my bag. In the early weeks, I mostly bring in sensory play for us to share. This might be playdough, kinetic sand, clay, or crazy soap. I often have a story-book, and sometimes, I will also have food to share. Sometimes, we will be inside, and other times outside, and we play. The child takes the lead, and we explore, share, and enjoy being with one another. During this time, I am watching and holding the space for the child; I am noticing how they react, their facial expressions, their noises, and their body language. Sometimes, I might comment on this, 'Ooo, I am wondering if you are really enjoying the feel of the sand; I can see you are laughing and smiling.' Within this play, when it feels appropriate, we will talk about feelings and emotions, but this is always led by how the child responds and reacts. The first few weeks of my job are to connect and get to know the child, to come alongside them, learn about them, build a relationship with them, and help them to feel safe. Part of helping them feel safe is not to bombard them with questions but to notice, be playful, and enjoy being in their company. Because I work with children for a school year, I have the luxury of time and space to go slowly and get to know them. Over the year, the work will adapt and change based on what the child needs. You can find more information on this work in my book *Supporting Children with Social, Emotional and Mental Health Needs in the Early Years*[41].

Outdoors

There is growing research into how being outside is a boost to our well-being and mental health. A growing number of GPs are now prescribing outdoor groups such as gardening/running/walking before they suggest medication for some patients struggling with their mental health. It is believed that spending ten minutes outside can be enough to lower our stress levels. I know that I find being outside a massive boost to my wellbeing. I garden, walk, and cold water swim all year round. When I am feeling highly stressed, I know that if I can be outside in water, my stress levels will significantly lower. It's incredible how healing I find cold water to be. I am not suggesting everyone takes up cold water swimming (but if you want to know more, I have some info in the further reading section). Just for a moment, think about your experience of being outside. Do you get outside much/enough? Being outside and engaging with nature doesn't have to be going to a beach or a forest; it can simply be walking in a park, walking under trees along the street, noticing the flowers in people's gardens as you walk to work, or growing plants in a window box. In the winter, I work hard to bring the outside in, I plant bulbs inside the house to have some early spring colour, and I buy daffodils when they first arrive in supermarkets to bring some colour and joy into the house.

The impact of being outside on our wellbeing is the same for children as it is for adults. Most of the children I work with are a lot happier, calmer, and engaged when they are outside. It is important that we give our outdoor spaces as much attention as we give to our indoor spaces. There is an excellent book by Sarah Watkins, *Outdoor Play for Healthy Minds*[42]; this book is full of practical suggestions and ideas on how you can utilise the outdoors to boost children's wellbeing.

DOI: 10.4324/9781032692944-22

CASE EXAMPLE

Robbie found being in the classroom a huge challenge; he didn't like sitting on the carpet, and he would wriggle and poke others around him. He was often overwhelmed when he was in the classroom, and his response to this was to be very quiet, often silent; in the classroom, he was mostly selectively mute. But outside, Robbie was a different boy; he smiled and laughed and talked to adults and children. He enjoyed counting and collecting leaves and seeds he found on the ground. He was hugely knowledgeable about the environment and was able to name the trees, plants, and animals around the outdoor space. Robbie was a farmer's son; when he was at home, most of his time was spent outside helping his parents on the farm. He knew how to milk cows, how to collect eggs, and how to talk to a horse as you approached it. Robbie loved the outdoors; he knew how to lift up leaves carefully to look for bugs. He was such a gentle, caring boy. Fortunately, Robbie went to a village primary school with a fantastic outside space, and the staff quickly realised they needed to give him as much opportunity as they could for him to engage in his learning outside. They would often do reading, phonics, and number work with him outside. I was privileged to work with Robbie for his reception year, all our nurture work was based outside, and I learnt so much from Robbie about cows, names of plants, and where to look for hens' eggs when they are playing tricks on you.

SEMH

SEMH stands for social, emotional, and mental health. We all have SEMH needs, and on some days, these needs are higher than on other days. Just for a moment, think about your SEMH needs, do a mini health check, and think about how you are. As I am writing this, it is a Sunday morning at the end of week three of the new school year, and I am tired. My work has been quite challenging; the step back into the school year is always a bit of a shock! But this year, it feels a bit harder; I'm not sure why. My SEMH isn't as high as it usually is, I am feeling a little intolerant of those close to me (my husband and daughter who live with me!), I am feeling a little tired of being with people. I saw friends yesterday, and it was lovely, but by the end of the day, I'd had enough. These are all signs to me that I need to take extra care. I had a cold water swim at the end of work on Thursday, which helped, and this afternoon, I am going to plant bulbs in the garden; I know that will help, too. As I have mentioned throughout this book, I work in the world of children with high SEMH needs. I love the job, but giving attention to my SEMH needs is vital, too. Before we continue, just think for a moment about what helps your SEMH needs. It will be different on different days. The following are a few suggestions, and further reading on this can be found in my book *Promoting Emotional Wellbeing in Early Years Staff* [43]:

Having enough sleep
Eating well
Being outside
Exercising
Connecting with others
Resting
Being creative

DOI: 10.4324/9781032692944-23

Self-compassion

I think this subject is one of the most important areas in wellbeing. Many adults and a growing number of children can be hugely negative to themselves, with an inner dialogue of negativity. Self-compassion is about being kind to ourselves and being compassionate to ourselves. If we do something wrong, make a mistake, or forget something, instead of telling ourselves negative words or being self-critical, we need to learn to be kind, gentle, and understanding with ourselves. One of the leading writers in this area is Dr Kristin Neff. I found her first book, *Self-Compassion*[44], to be a hugely influential book. It taught me how to change my inner negative script. It took me a while, but I have successfully changed my negative inner script to one that is much gentler, kinder, and compassionate.

A PRACTITIONER'S VIEW

We can model being self-compassionate to the children we work with. If we do something wrong, we can say out loud, '*Oh, I made a mistake there, but that is okay. Next time, I can do it differently.*' If we hear children saying that they are stupid or rubbish (I hear this regularly), we can gently say, '*That is sad that you think that. It's okay to not be able to do something; there are so many other things you can do. I'd like to help you love yourself and what you are good at.*' A beautiful book to share with children is *I Am Enough* by Grace Byers[45].

DOI: 10.4324/9781032692944-24

Self-harm

This section needs a warning with it, as it is a difficult subject. If this feels too hard to read right now, then please look after yourself and jump to the next section. Self-harm is when someone intentionally hurts or injures their body. We often think about self-harm with older children and adults, but it does occur in younger children, too. I have worked with young children who were regularly self-harming. This is an area which may be relevant to the children, staff, or parents you work with. For further information on self-harm and how to signpost and support adults and older children, I would suggest looking at the NHS website[46] and the Mind website[47]. I have also added further links in the further reading section.

A PRACTITIONER'S VIEW

If you think a child you are working with is self-harming, have a conversation with the parents about the behaviours you are seeing and find out if they are also seeing this at home. Suggest to the parents that they speak to the GP. You may also want to contact the child's health visitor and your Area SENCO. As we have said in earlier sections, behaviour is a form of communication; the child is letting us know they are very unhappy about something, and we need to take this seriously and support them. It may be that the behaviour is caused by the child being fearful and anxious; there may be some big changes happening in their lives currently. We, of course, also need to question if this is a child protection issue and make the relevant referrals if we think that might be the case. If it is not a child protection issue, you

DOI: 10.4324/9781032692944-25

may want to consider an early help referral. For more information on self-harm in children, look at the NSPCC website[48]. If you are working with a child who is self-harming, this can be very difficult and emotive for the adults. The staff must have support through supervision to manage any feelings that occur through this. It is also important to signpost parents/carers to places for support. This could be through health visitors or websites such as the NSPCC, as mentioned previously, or Action for Children, which has a page with advice for parents on their website[49]

Self-esteem

Self-esteem is about how we view and value ourselves. It is about the beliefs we have about who we are, what we can do, and what we are good at. Sometimes, on social media, we can be led to believe that all we need to do is repeat positive affirmations and positive comments about ourselves, and our self-esteem will be boosted and fine. Sadly, for many people, it's not that simple. I find the whole positive affirmation comments a bit sickly and shallow. There is a quote on Mind's website[50] that says, 'For me, low self-esteem is the little voice inside my head that says "you're rubbish, you're fat, what's the point, you're not cut out for this" and so on . . .'. If those are the messages you hear in your head, then positive affirmations are unlikely to change that. I think self-compassion (as mentioned in an earlier section) is so important for someone with low self-esteem. What follows are some suggestions on how we can support ourselves if we have low self-esteem:

- Be kind to yourself. When you hear yourself saying negative things, try and change that script and say kind things to yourself, e.g., *'It's okay I got that wrong, it's just a mistake, or I know it is hard, but I can do it.'* Imagine you were talking to a friend; usually, the words we use for a friend are much kinder than the words we use for ourselves
- Do something that brings you moments of joy, that might be going for a walk, baking a cake, seeing a friend, or gardening
- Think about those things you enjoy, the things that are important to you, maybe making a photo mood board or writing down ideas. I have three photo boards on my desktop: one on happiness, one on hope, and one on gratitude. These are on my desktop to remind me when I am feeling low of the things that are important to me and that bring me joy

DOI: 10.4324/9781032692944-26

A PRACTITIONER'S VIEW

Young children can also have low self-esteem. Sometimes, we see this through them refusing to try something new, becoming dysregulated when they can't do something, or sometimes we hear them vocalising self-critical thoughts. We can support them by being gentle, reassuring them it is okay to get things wrong, acknowledging how they are feeling, and reminding them of times when they have managed something.

Selective mutism

Selective mutism is a form of anxiety which prevents the child/adult from speaking in certain situations. Sometimes, this only becomes apparent when the child starts nursery or school. They may speak at home and with family all the time, but in the school/nursery, they do not speak. Sometimes, families are very surprised when they hear their child is never speaking in the education setting. It is vital to get early support for the child when you become aware of selective mutism. First, have a conversation with the family, find out if there are other places/contexts where the child doesn't speak, and make a referral through the local speech and language team. In the referral, say that you think it might be selective mutism. In our area, we have a specialist selective mutism speech and language therapist on the team who is able to work with the child and offer advice to the parent and education setting.

It is really important that everyone understands this is coming from a place of anxiety; it is not about chosen behaviours or the child being a bit shy or rude. I have had some practitioners take it personally that the child doesn't talk to them or in the setting, as if the child has taken a dislike to them. This is not about them; it is about the child being so anxious they can't speak. As well as making a referral, it is a good idea to become informed about this area. A great place to start is on the selective mutism website[51]. In the further reading section, I have suggested a few other links and suggestions, too.

DOI: 10.4324/9781032692944-27

Self-regulation

In many ways, self-regulation is a complex set of skills that some expect children to have from a young age. Self-regulation is partly about being able to regulate how we feel and how we behave, but it is also about being aware of how our behaviour impacts others. To be able to stay calm when we are feeling cross, we need to have self-awareness and cognitive functioning that enables us to think about doing something that calms us in the moment of rage or fear. I can think of many adults who find that hard, so I find it baffling that we expect young children to be able to master this.

The way that children learn to self-regulate is by having a calm and gentle adult alongside them to co-regulate with them. The adult can show them strategies that can help them find calmness. Being dysregulated is incredibly scary for the child (and sometimes adults find this frightening to see in children). Being able to self-regulate is such a vital skill, but it is one that children need support in learning; they won't just naturally do it or learn it by themselves. Having an emotionally rich environment where we are regularly talking about emotions, naming emotions, and recognising that emotions are neither negative nor positive – they just are what they are – are all vital ways to support a child with learning the skills for self-regulation. For more on self-regulation I recommend Tamsin Grimmer and Wendy Geens' book, *Nurturing Self-Regulation in Early Childhood.*[52]

DOI: 10.4324/9781032692944-28

Spiritual wellbeing

In the UK, we don't talk about spiritual wellbeing that often. It doesn't get the attention that other aspects of wellbeing do. When I wrote a book on supporting emotional wellbeing in staff[53], one chapter of that book was about spiritual wellbeing. At the time of writing it, I was looking at several different definitions of wellbeing. One was from New Zealand, called Hauora, which is a Maori view of health and wellbeing and covers physical, mental, social, and spiritual aspects. I really liked their description of spiritual wellbeing[54]:

> Taha wairua (spiritual wellbeing): The values and beliefs that help people decide the way they live, the search for meaning and purpose in life, and personal identity and self-awareness.
>
> (Paragraph 4)

Often, we think of spiritual wellbeing as being linked to a faith-based practice, but it is more than that; it is about feeling connected and having a sense of being part of something bigger than ourselves. Some people find this through faith-based practices, attending places of worship, prayer, and reading holy books. Others find this through connecting with the outdoors, contemplative practices such as mindfulness and yoga, practices of silence, and practices of gratitude. I think having a spiritual practice is a really crucial part of our wellbeing toolkit, and it is one we can offer and share with children. One simple way we can do that is through sharing the awe and wonder of being in nature, noticing and connecting ourselves to something bigger than ourselves.

DOI: 10.4324/9781032692944-29

Stress

We all need a little bit of stress to function each day; it helps us to get out of the house and go to work. Stress is not necessarily a negative thing, but unfortunately, we can allow it to build up, and a build-up of stress in our bodies can be extremely negative. Our bodies are amazing at telling us when we are stressed, but we are not always very good at hearing that or taking notice. Just for a moment, think about how your body tells you when you are stressed. For me, it is in my shoulders and neck. If I get a migraine, I know it has got too much, but before that, I get tension in my shoulders and neck. Stress can have a negative impact on all of our lives, from impacting our physical and mental health to affecting our relationships and our ability to work. It is so important that we take stress seriously. In 2020, Brene Brown did a podcast interview with two women called Emily and Amelia Nagosaki[55]; their interview was about different ways we can complete the stress cycle. Their thinking is that we all experience stress daily and need to find ways daily of releasing it; if we don't, it builds up in our bodies and makes us ill. They have a menu of suggestions on how we can do this. These include:

- Time in nature
- Laughing
- Crying
- Creative practice
- Exercise
- Affection – 6-second kiss, 20-second hug
- Connection with others

SSTEW scale

SSTEW stands for Sustained Shared Thinking and Emotional Wellbeing Scale for 2–5-year-olds. It was developed by Iram Siraj, Denise Kingston, and Edward Melhuish. It covers the following areas:

- Building trust
- Confidence and independence
- Social and emotional wellbeing
- Supporting and extending language and communication
- Supporting learning and critical thinking
- Assessing learning and language

The scales assess practice on seven levels, which go from inadequate to excellent. At the point of writing this book, an updated book is being published about how to use this scale, and as part of the update, they have extended it to be used with children aged 2–6 years[56]. This scale is used in the UK and widely internationally. This scale is another useful tool to use in our practice. It fits well with many of the other tools I have suggested, such as *Birth to Five Matters*[25]. However, the authors of the scale recommend that anyone thinking of using it attends a training session first for guidance on how to use it. For more information on this, you can find an interview with the writers on Early Years TV[57].

DOI: 10.4324/9781032692944-31

Thrive

Thrive is a trauma-informed assessment tool used to support the mental health and wellbeing of children and young people. It is used by many schools and early years settings across the country as a whole setting approach. This means many schools and early years settings will use the Thrive assessment tool to assess all the children, helping them to understand where there may be any underlying SEMH gaps for the children. The team I work with use Thrive in our daily work, and it is used in all the schools in the Bath area. Alongside the assessment tool is a training package to support the practitioners. You can find out more information about Thrive on their website[58].

DOI: 10.4324/9781032692944-32

Transitions

We all experience transitions daily, and for most adults and children, this is something that is barely thought about and is not a problem. However, for some children, transitions can be a tricky and stressful experience. Just for a moment, think about how many transitions the children you work with experience in a day, from waking to the time they end with you. You may be surprised at the number when you break it down. For some children, transitions are so overwhelming, and they may become distressed or refuse to engage in the transition. A question I often ask staff is whether all the transitions are necessary. Of course, some are, but in your review of transitions, you may find they are not all necessary, and you may be able to remove some of them. One of the key areas to supporting children with transitions is preparation. Often, we think about preparing children for big transitions such as moving to school, going on a trip, and having a new baby in the house, and this is important. We also need to think about smaller transitions and how we support children with these, those moments from pre-warnings before tidy-up time or putting their coats on, using visual timetables and now and next boards. We often think about using these resources for children with SEND needs, but we also need to think about these for children with SEMH needs. Actually, I would argue they are useful for all children. Kerry Murphy and Fifi Benham's book[59] has some excellent ideas and resources that might be useful, and I wrote a book[60] looking at the many different types of transitions and how we can support children, from the small to the major life-changing transitions.

DOI: 10.4324/9781032692944-33

CASE EXAMPLE

Dougie finds transitions very challenging. He has experienced lots of changes in his short life, having moved house four times in the last two years, and he is now attending his fifth education setting. Before he started his new school, he had a photo sheet of all the staff who were in his class. He has two teachers who share the teaching during the week. Each morning, he looks at the sheet with his mum to see which teacher is in that day. When he first arrives at school, the teaching assistant always welcomes him and takes him to do an activity, such as playing a game or looking at a story. This helps Dougie arrive and connect with an adult he trusts and hopefully enables him to have a calm start to the school day. During the day, the staff each have a visual timetable on a key fob that they carry around. They can use this to assist Dougie if he needs a little reminder of what is about to happen next; they also use a now and next board to assist in the preparation. In the class, they use some bells to give a 5-minute warning of tidy-up time. The staff always speaks to Dougie just before the bells ring to give him an additional warning. The preparation around lunchtime can often take a while, with children needing to wash hands, find lunch boxes, and line up; Dougie finds this very tricky and often becomes very dysregulated. Now, at the start of the lunch preparation, Dougie washes his hands first and then does a job with his TA; sometimes, they collect the lunch list, and other times, they get pencils out ready for the afternoon. It doesn't matter what the job is; the important thing is that Dougie does not have to sit and wait and become agitated before moving to lunchtime. These are all small examples and not at all difficult to put into place, but they make a significant difference in Dougie having a calm and regulated day. Of course, it doesn't always work, but often it does.

Wellbeing

It seems slightly strange to be writing a definition of wellbeing at this point, as we are close to the end of this section! But it is an A-Z of definitions, and, of course, W comes near the end! There are many definitions of wellbeing, but my definition of wellbeing is:

- Feeling loved
- Feeling safe
- Feeling that I belong
- Loving myself
- Feeling good about who I am
- Being able to cope with life's difficulties

Just for a moment, think about this for yourself.

Then, take a moment and think about this for the children you work with. You may want to identify one or two.

With this definition in mind, do you think they have a good wellbeing?

One important aspect of wellbeing is a sense that we belong. It is so important that every child we work with feels they belong in our setting. There are many ways we can support this, through making sure we know them and their family well, knowing the names of their family, knowing their likes and dislikes, but also by them seeing examples of themselves and their family around them, through images, books, and toys.

Throughout this definition section, there are many examples of what can impact our and our children's wellbeing but also what can support all of our wellbeing. In the next section, I explore in more depth how we can support our wellbeing and encourage our colleagues in this, too.

DOI: 10.4324/9781032692944-34

Window of tolerance

The term 'window of tolerance' originally came from Dan Siegel[61]. It is a model that describes when we are able to cope. We all have times in our lives where we are able to cope, these are known as windows of tolerance. When we are in the window of tolerance we can cope with everyday challenges, difficulties, and everyday life occurrences. We can cope with new information, and instructions and we can make decisions. Within our window of tolerance, there will be some ups and downs, we all experience these, but everyone's window of tolerance is different, for some, their window is much narrower. When we move outside our window of tolerance we can find it very difficult to cope with the everyday challenges, taking instructions and making decisions.

Just for a moment, think about a time you have been outside your window of tolerance. If I haven't had enough sleep, my window of tolerance narrows; I am very intolerant of my family and find myself snapping, and I can find it hard to make a decision.

I find this model so helpful for explaining to staff and parents why children behave in certain ways. If a child is not coping with the small transitions, the normal everyday practice of their routine, they are showing us their window of tolerance that day is much narrower, and we need to adapt to support them. There are many things that can impact how big or small our window of tolerance is, for example, stress, life changes, illness, lack of sleep, poor diet, and challenging relationships with others; these can all make our windows smaller. But there are also things that can make our window bigger: minimal stress, experiences of joy, achievement or mastery of something, and supportive relationships can help to build resilience and increase the window of tolerance. As adults working with children, we want to aim to build and strengthen each child's window of tolerance. There is a useful YouTube video from Hampshire Child and Adolescent Mental Health Service explaining the window of tolerance in more detail[62].

DOI: 10.4324/9781032692944-35

Conclusion of Section 1

I hope the first section has been useful in giving you a brief overview of many of the key terms used in the field of wellbeing. Below is a list of further ideas and suggestions of places to look and websites linked with each of the above definitions. Some of the links are for resources for adults, and some are for resources for children.

DOI: 10.4324/9781032692944-36

Further reading/links

Anxiety

Adults

Anxiety UK. https://www.anxietyuk.org.uk/.
Haig, M. (2021) *The comfort book*. Edinburgh: Canongate publishers.
Smith, J. (2022) *Why has nobody told me this before*. London: Penguin.
Wax, R. (2014) *Sane new world*. London: Hodder books.

Children

Bright, R. (2020) *Worrysaurus*. London: Orchard books.
Karst, P. (2001) *The invisible string*. Camarillo: Devorss publishers.
Morrisroe, R. (2022) *The Drama Llama: A story about soothing anxiety*. London: Puffin.
Percival, T. (2018) *Ruby's worry*. London: Bloomsbury books.

ACEs

Adults

Sterne, A. & Poole, L. (2009) *Domestic violence and children.* Abingdon: Routledge.

Van Der Kolk, B. (2014) *The body keeps the score.* London: Viking.

A wide range of resources from Beacon House, who specialise in trauma. https://beaconhouse.org.uk/resources/.

Winfrey. O. & Perry, B. (2021) *What happened to you? Conversations on trauma resilience and healing.* London: Bluebird.

Children

Conkbayir, M. (2023) *Maya's ACE adventures: A story to celebrate children's resilience following adverse childhood experiences.* Abingdon: Routledge.

Conkbayir, M. (2023) *Nurturing children's resilience following adverse childhood experiences an adult guide.* Abingdon: Routledge.

Lawler, C. & Howes, N. (2022) *Luna little legs: Helping young children to understand domestic abuse and coercive control.* Abingdon: Routledge.

Milner, K. (2017) *My name is not refugee.* Edinburgh: Barrington Stoke Publisher.

Milner, K. (2019) *It's a no money day.* Edinburgh: Barrington Stoke Publisher.

Attachment needs

Adults

Delahooke, M. (2020) Beyond behaviours: Using brain science and compassion to understand and solve children's behavioural challenges. London: Sheldon press.

Delahooke, M. (2022) *Brain-body parenting: How to stop managing behaviour and start raising joyful, resilient kids.* London: Sheldon press.

Golding, K. & Hughes, D. (2012) *Creating loving attachments: Parenting with PACE to nurture confidence and security in the troubled child.* London: Jessica Kingsly Publishers.

Children

Appelt, K. (2006) *O my baby, my little one.* London: Clarion books.

Karst, P. (2001) *The invisible string.* Camarillo: Devorss publishers.

Creativity/imagination

Adults

Brand, L. (2022) *The joy journal for adults.* London: Bluebird.

Reggio Children website. https://www.reggiochildren.it/en/reggio-emilia-approach/100-linguaggi-en/.

Sakr, M., Trivedy, B., Hall, N., O'Brien, L. & Federici, R. (2018) *Creativity and making in early childhood.* London: Bloomsbury.

Thornton, L. & Brunton, P. *Understanding the Reggio approach.* Abingdon: Routledge.

Children

Altés, M. (2020) *I am an artist*. London: Macmillan children's book.

Beaty, A. (2021) *Aaron slater illustrator*. New York: Abram's books for young readers.

Brand, L. (2020) *The joy journal for magical everyday play*. London: Bluebird.

Reynolds, P. (2004) *The dot*. London: Walker Books.

Robinson, N. (2022) *I am an artist*. London: Starfish bay children's book.

Depression

Adults

Haig, M. (2015) *Reasons to stay alive*. Edinburgh: Canongate publishers.

NHS How to help someone with depression. https://www.nhs.uk/mental-health/advice-for-life-situations-and-events/how-to-help-someone-with-depression/.

Smith, J. (2022) *Why has nobody told me this before?* London: Penguin.

Wax, R. (2016) *A mindfulness guide for the frazzled*. London: Penguin.

Children

Bright, R. (2019) *Worrysaurus*. London: Orchard books.

Eland, E. (2020) *When sadness comes to call*. London: Anderson Press.

Lloyd Jones, L. B. (2015) *The princess and the fog*. London: Jessica Kingsley Publishers.

Peters, A. F. & Peters, P. (2014) *The colour thief*. London: Wayland books.

Dysregulation

Adults

Grimmer, T. & Geens, W. (2022) *Nurturing self-regulation in early childhood*. Abingdon: Routledge.
Sunderland, M. (2016) *What every parent needs to know*. London: Dorling Kindersley.

Children

Bright, R. (2022) *The Stompysaurus*. London: Orchard books.
Percival, T. (2019) *Ravis roar*. London: Bloomsbury books.

Early intervention

Adults

Hub of Hope website, informing you of what support is available in your area. https://hubofhope.co.uk/.
Whalley, M. & Arnold, C. (2013) *Working with families in children's centres and early years settings*. Abingdon: Routledge.

Emotional regulation

Adults

Grimmer, T. (2022) *Supporting behaviour and emotions in the early years*. Abingdon: Routledge.

Grimmer, T. & Geens, W. (2022) *Nurturing self-regulation in early childhood*. Abingdon: Routledge.

Sunderland, M. (2016) *What every parent needs to know*. London: Dorling Kindersley.

Children

Bright, R. (2022) *The Stompysaurus*. London: Orchard books.

Emotional literacy

Adults

Allingham, S. (2020) *Emotional literacy in the early years: Helping children balance body and mind*. Salisbury: Practical pre-school books.

Gilbert, L., Gus, L. & Rose, J. (2021) *Emotion coaching with children and young people in schools*. London: Jessica Kingsley Publishers.

Children

Emotion rollers for play dough. https://www.yellow-door.net/products/lets-roll-emotions/.

Llenas, A. (2016) *The colour monster*. London: Templar publishing.
Parr, T. (2009) *The feelings book*. London: Little Brown young readers.
Parr, T. (2010) *Feelings flash cards*. San Francisco: Chronicle books.
Walden, L. (2018) *Feelings inside my heart and my head*. London: Caterpillar books.

Enabling environment

Adults

Bryce-Clegg, A. (2013) *Continuous provision in the early years*. Lancashire: Featherstone.
Ephgrave, A. (2018) *Planning in the moment with young children: A practical guide for early years practitioners and parents*. Abingdon: Routledge.
Smith, K. (2022) *Bringing Hygge into the early years A step by step guide to bring a calm and slow approach to your teaching*. Abingdon: Routledge.

Fight/flight/freeze/fawn

Adults

Conkbayir, M. (2022) *The neuroscience of the developing child*. Abingdon: Routledge.
Mainstone-Cotton, S. (2021) *Supporting children with social, emotional and mental health needs in the early years*. Abingdon: Routledge.
Useful videos explaining fight/flight/freeze on CAMHS website. https://www.camhs-resources.co.uk/videos.

Holistic development

Adults

Brodie, K. (2018) *The holistic care and development of children from birth to three.* Abingdon: Routledge.

Zero to three. https://www.zerotothree.org/.

Listening to children

Adults

Ephgrave, A. (2018) *Planning in the moment with young children: A practical guide for early years practitioners and parents.* Abingdon. Routledge.

Mainstone-Cotton, S. (2019) *Listening to young children in early years settings: A practical guide.* London: Jessica Kingsley Publishers.

Loving Pedagogy

Adults

Bradbury, A. & Grimmer, T. (2024) *Love and nurture in the early years.* London: Sage.

Golding, K. & Hughes, D. (2012) *Creating loving attachments: Parenting with PACE to nurture confidence and security in the troubled child.* London: Jessica Kingsly Publishers.

Grimmer, T. (2021) *Developing a loving pedagogy in the early years: How love fits with professional practice.* Abingdon: Routledge.

Children

Bright, R. (2020) *Love monster*. London: Harper Collins.
Cooke, T. (2019) *So much*. London: Walker books.
Cooke, T. (2020) *Full, full, full of love*. London: Walker books.
McBratney, S. (2014) *Guess how much I love you*. London: Walker books.

Joyfulness

Adults

Cotton, F. (2017) *Finding joy in every day and letting go of perfect*. London: Orion spring publisher.
Kingston-Hughes, B. (2024) *Why children need joy: The fundamental truth about childhood*. London: Sage.
Nichols, W. (2018) *Blue mind how water makes you happier, more connected and better at what you do*. London: Abacus.
Wild swimming information. https://outdoorswimmer.com/featured/a-beginners-guide-to-wild-swimming/.

Children

Atinuke. (2012) *Anna Hibiscus song*. London: Walker books.
Bard, M. (2023) *Be happy! A little book of mindfulness*. London: Templar publishing.

Nature deficit disorder

Adults

Barnes, J. (2020) *50 Fantastic ideas for forest school.* Lancashire: Featherstone.
Cree, J. (2021) *The essential guide to forest school and nature pedagogy.* Abingdon: Routledge.
Wildlife Trust has free nature spotting sheets and activity ideas. https://www.wildlifewatch.org.uk/activities.

Children

Carlisle, E. (2023) *What do you see when you look at a tree?* London: Big Picture Press.
Davies, N. (2020) *My butterfly bouquet.* London: Wren and Rook.
Murray, L. (2023) *The girl who loves bugs.* London: Macmillan books.

Nurture

Bradbury, A. & Grimmer, T. (2024) *Love and nurture in the early years.* London: Sage.
Delahooke, M. (2020) *Beyond behaviours: Using brain science and compassion to understand and solve children's behavioural challenges.* London: Sheldon Press.
Delahooke, M. (2022) *Brain-body parenting: How to stop managing behaviour and start raising joyful, resilient kids.* London: Sheldon Press.

Outdoors

Adults

An education toolkit for early years outdoor ideas. https://worldforumfoundation.org/wp-content/uploads/2018/08/Educator_Toolkit__ENG.pdf.

Bryce-Clegg, A. & Wotherspoon, O. (2023) *Creating spaces to play outdoors*. London: Bloomsbury.

Children

De la Prada, S. (2020) *National trust: 50 things to do before you are 11 3/4. An outdoor adventure handbook*. London: Noisy Crow.

Hegarty, P. (2015) *Tree*. London: Little Tiger kids.

SEMH

Adults

Hammond, C. (2020) *The art of rest*. Edinburgh: Cannongate.

Walker, M. (2018) *Why we sleep*. London: Penguin.

Children

Hoffman, S. (2018) *Yoga for kids*. London: DK children.

Kinder, W. (2019) *Mindfulness for kids*. London: DK children.

Mood flip book. (2020) *Help kids to identify and manage their emotions*. Hampshire: Peter Pauper Press.

Self-compassion

Adults

Brown, B. (2022) *The gifts of imperfection*. Minnesota: Hazeldon publishing.
Website. https://self-compassion.org/.

Children

Hoffman, M. (2007) *Amazing grace*. London: Francis Lincoln Publishers.
Love, J. (2019) *Julian is a mermaid*. London: Walker books.

Self-harm

NHS guidance for parents. https://www.england.nhs.uk/blog/advice-for-parents-guardians-and-carers-on-how-to-support-a-child-or-young-person-if-youre-concerned-about-their-mental-health/.
Young Minds website. https://www.youngminds.org.uk/young-person/blog/five-things-you-can-do-if-someone-tells-you-they-are-self-harming/.

Self-esteem

Adults

Neff, K. (2011) *Self compassion*. London: Hodder & Stoughton.
Smith, J. (2022) *Why has nobody told me this before*. London: Penguin.

Children

Bright, R. (2020) *Wobblysaurus*. London: Orchard books.

Selective Mutism

Adults

Johnson, M. & Wintgens, A. (2016) *The selective mutism resource manual* (second ed.). Abingdon: Speechmark publishing.
Rae Smith, B. & Sluckin, A. (2014) *Tackling selective mutism a guide for professionals and parents*. London: Jessica Kingsley Publishers.

Children

Johnson, M. & Wintgens, A. (2012) *Can I tell you about selective mutism?* London: Jessica Kingsley Publishers.
Maskell, C. (2017) *The loudest roar: A book about selective mutism*. London: Create Space Independent Publishing Platform.

Self-regulation

Adults

Foundation years LED events: Self-regulation in the early years – Dr Suzanne Zeedyk. www.youtube.com/watch?v=8ng3UfkdaIM.

Children

Cain, J. (2021) *The way I feel*. Chicago: Parenting Press.

Spiritual wellbeing

Adults

Allen, R. (2022) *Grounded: How connection with nature can improve our mental and physical wellbeing*. London: Wellbeck publishing.
Maitland, S. (2008) *A book of silence*. London: Granta Books.
Williams, M. & Penman, D. (2011) *Mindfulness a practical guide to finding peace in a frantic world*. London: Piatkus books.

Children

Edwards, N. & Hickey, K. (2019) *Happy a children's book of mindfulness*. London: Caterpillar books.
Hutts Aston, D (2023) *A shell is cozy*. San Francisco: Chronicle books.

Stress

Adults

Mate, G. (2019) *When the body says no the cost of hidden stress*. London: Vermilion.
Nagoski, E. & Nagoski, A. (2020) *Burn out solve your stress cycle*. London: Vermillon.

Transition

Adults

Allingham, S. (2015) *Transitions in the early years: A practical guide to supporting children between early years settings and key stage 1.* Salisbury: Practical Preschool.

O'Connor, A. (2017) *Understanding transitions in the early years: Supporting change through attachment and resilience.* Abingdon: Routledge.

Children

Altes, M. (2020) *My new home.* London: Macmillan children's book.

Civardi, A. (2021) *Going to school.* London: Usborne.

Civardi, A. (2021) *Moving house.* London: Usborne.

Fuller, R. (2009) *My new baby.* Swindon: Child's play international.

Wellbeing

Adults

Chatterjee, R. (2018) *The stress solution the 4 steps to a calmer, happier, healthier you.* London: Penguin.

Smith, J. (2022) *Why has nobody told me this before.* London: Penguin.

Children

Adeola, D. (2021) *Hey you an empowering celebration of growing up black*. London: Puffin.

Edwards, N. (2019) *Happy: A children's book of mindfulness*. London: Caterpillar books.

Window of tolerance

Jersey government info on window of tolerance. https://www.gov.je/ SiteCollectionDocuments/Education/ID%20The%20Window%20 of%20Tolerance%2020%2006%2016.pdf.

Embedding wellbeing practices

Section 1 of this book gave you some brief overviews of the many different aspects of wellbeing. I hope it was able to offer some clarity around words and terms that can sometimes appear confusing.

This section of the book looks at how we can embed wellbeing practices into our daily work. It will offer some practical ideas and suggestions. The areas this section is looking at are:

- The rights of the child in relation to wellbeing
- The role of the adult in relation to wellbeing
- How the adult can prioritise their and their colleagues' wellbeing
- How we can create an enabling environment which promotes wellbeing
- How we can engage parents and work in partnership with them when supporting their children's wellbeing
- How to write a wellbeing policy
- Signposting for further advice
- Staff training

The rights of the child in relation to wellbeing

When we think about the rights of the child, the first place to start is the United Nations Convention on the Rights of the Child (UNCRC); this is a crucial convention which has 54 articles in it that cover all areas of a child's life. The UNCRC states that every child has rights 'without discrimination of any kind, irrespective of the child's or his or her parent's or legal guardians race, colour, sex, language, political or other opinion, national ethnic or social origin, property, disability, birth or other status' (This is on their website, on page 1).[63] There are four articles in the UNCRC that are described as special articles as they are the general principles, these are:

Non discrimination (article 2)
The best interest of the child (article 3)
Right to life survival and development (article 6)
Right to be listened to (article 12)

The UNCRC has been signed by 196 countries; currently, the United States of America has not signed it. All the countries that have signed are held to account by the UN and need to submit regular reports to the UN about how they are holding up children's rights. In the UK, other agencies also submit reports; for example, charities. The UN then gives feedback on these reports and recommendations on how things can be improved. You can find more info on this on the UNICEF website[64]. UNICEF also has a section for children on their website[65] and an excellent children's book[66] explaining to children about their rights.

So, how does this fit with wellbeing? The articles are all varied, but fundamentally, they are about ensuring every child has the best start to life. I am going to look at the four leading articles and briefly think about how this applies to our work with wellbeing and children. I am taking the words for each article from the children's version, as mentioned previously[67].

DOI: 10.4324/9781032692944-39

Non discrimination (article 2)

This article is about every child, no matter where they live, whether they are a boy or girl, whether they have a disability, whether they are rich or poor, no matter who their parents are and what they believe or don't believe. No child should be treated unfairly for any reason. So, how do we do this in our practice? It is about making sure every child, family, and staff member feels that they belong. We want all our settings to be a place where everyone feels represented and see examples of others like them. We do this through the books we use, the toys we have, and the images we use, but this is not enough; we also need to ensure we are curious, interested, and welcoming to everyone but also questioning our own practice. This is not an easy, quick win; we need to dig deep and ask difficult questions. There are two books I recommend reading that may help in this process: Valerie Daniel[67] has written an excellent book called *Anti-Racist Practice in the early years*. This is an accessible book that challenges, supports, and guides all of us. The other book I have found helpful is Kerry Murphy's *Supporting the Wellbeing of children with SEND.*[68]

The best interest of the child (article 3)

This article is about ensuring that when adults make decisions, they must think about how their decisions will affect children. All adults should do what is best for children. Governments need to ensure that children are protected and looked after by their parents or by others when needed, and governments need to make sure that people and places looking after children are doing a good job. So, how do we do this in our practice? This links to the decisions we referred to previously around making sure we think about how all children are welcomed and represented. It is also around our safeguarding practices and how we protect children, but also being curious about what the child is telling us through their behaviour, remembering all behaviour is a form of communication. I also think this is around how we do our planning for children and how we ensure we are meeting the needs and interests of every child. I am a big fan of Anna Ephgrave's work *Planning in the moment with young children*[69]. This book helps us to think about how we can actively put into action meeting the best interest of every child.

Right to life survival and development (article 6)

This article is about every child having a right to be alive and the need for governments to ensure that all children survive and develop. As I am writing this section of the book, this article feels particularly pertinent. Currently, the news is full of information about the deaths of children in the Middle East with Gaza, Israel, and Ukraine. It is so easy to take this article for granted; of course, all children have a right to life, but currently, we are reminded that far too many children don't get this. And also, in our own country, too many children's lives are being impacted by extreme poverty. The Rowntree Foundation report[70] in 2023 found that around one million children in the UK have experienced destitution. This is where families cannot meet the basic needs of warmth, staying dry, being fed, and staying clean. This has a huge impact on children's development. How do we respond to this? I think it is important that we know our families and communities, that we know where we can signpost families for help, and that we help families to know they don't need to feel shame if they are struggling financially. I know in some areas, nurseries and schools have links with food banks and food pantries, and sometimes, they also provide washing machine facilities.

Right to be listened to (article 12)

This article is about the right of all children to give their opinions on issues that affect them and for children to be involved in decision-making about things that affect them. This article underpins all our work; we all need to ensure we listen to children throughout our work. We know that listening to children is more than just hearing the words they might say; it is also listening to their behaviour, their facial expressions, and body language. It is about checking with them that we have correctly understood what we think we have heard. This is also about thinking about how we involve children in decisions that impact our planning, room layouts, the food and drink we offer, the activities and toys we provide, and how we recruit staff. To find out more ways we can involve children in decision making, you could have a look at my book *Listening to Young Children in early years settings*[29].

The role of the adult is crucial in supporting a child's wellbeing. We are in a unique position of spending a lot of time with children. For some children, we spend more time with them than their parents do. With this comes a huge responsibility to love, nurture, and help children feel safe and that they belong. In the previous section, under the description of wellbeing, I wrote my definition of wellbeing. I am going to look at each of these now in relation to how our role supports a child's wellbeing.

Feeling loved
Feeling safe
Feeling I belong
Loving myself (helping a child to love themself) and feeling good about who I am (helping a child to feel good about who they are and what they can do)
Being able to cope with life's difficulties

Feeling loved

I believe a child feeling loved by us is the underpinning core of our wellbeing practice. As I mentioned in the definitions part of the book, there is a phrase called professional love, which is a really helpful phrase to understand and use, particularly for people who feel uncomfortable with using the term love in our role. In this part of the chapter, I want to explore how I think we can show children that we love them and what that looks like in daily practice.

Knowing the child as part of loving them

In many settings, you will have key children you work with, or if you are in a school, this might be a whole class, or you may be a 1–1 teaching/ nursery assistant, or you may be a childminder or nanny working with a small number of children. I have nine children with whom I am currently working. Part of loving the child is knowing the child. What follows are a few questions you might want to think about in relation to the children you support:

Do you know who is in their family and what their household looks like? It might be different households on different days.
Do you know what makes the child happy?
Do you know what interests the child, what they like playing with, what fascinates them?
Do you know what makes the child sad?
Do they have pets? Or are there any animals they are particularly keen on?
Do you know when the child's birthday is?
Do you know what the child did on the weekend/days they weren't with you?

You may not know all the answers to these, and some things will change, but knowing these few things can help us to know the child. Remembering things like the child's pet or the name of their sibling can help the child to feel they have been thought of. We, of course, need to be sensitive as many of us work with children where home life is very difficult. I work with one child whose brother is extremely violent to him; it's important I remember this information if I am talking about home. When I know a family regularly goes to the park, or the child likes to play on her trampoline in the garden, I can ask about that and show an interest in that. It is all part of connecting; we like it when our friends remember things about us and enquire. It makes us feel remembered and important to them; it is the same with children. Another essential part of knowing what a child likes is including this in our planning. If I know I work with a child who loves animals and facts about animals, I use this in the work we do together.

Appropriate touch in our practice as part of loving them

There are many ways in which we need to use touch: when a child falls down, if a baby or toddler needs changing or picking up, if a child needs their hand holding. But there are also times when a child needs a cuddle, or some comfort on their arm, or their back being stroked, or they want to snuggle into you. Touch is so important; when we are touched in a loving, consensual, appropriate way, it can release positive chemicals in our brain that contribute to us feeling good about ourselves and feeling calm and safe. There was a time in the early years when there was a lot of fear around touching children and the fear of allegations against us. This brought about the idea and the practice in some places of not cuddling a child or gently touching them. Thankfully, in the UK, this seems to be significantly shifting. I think Tamsin Grimmer's book *Developing a Loving Pedagogy in the Early Years*[71] has gone a long way in helping practitioners with their reflection and thinking in this area.

Many of the children I work with can become dysregulated or highly anxious. Often, a gentle hand on their arm or gently stroking their back can help them to find calmness. We only do this with consent and with children that we know find this helpful, but it can make such a difference. I usually see the children I work with once a week, and it's not uncommon for some of those children to throw their arms around me with delight when I arrive; they are thrilled to see I have arrived, and the next question is often 'What is in your bag today?', as they know I always bring something in for us to play with. If I pushed those children away and dismissed their hugs, they would feel sad and rejected. Instead, I put my arm around them and tell them how delighted I am to see them, that seeing them has made me so happy.

Feeling safe

For many of the children I work with, they often don't feel safe. You may be surprised at this and wonder why a child wouldn't feel safe in your nursery or school. It is not because the nursery or school is unsafe as in unsafe practice, but it can be a strong feeling for many children. This is particularly the case for children who have experienced trauma, but many children who are neurodiverse may also feel unsafe. There are a few things that can help children to feel safe, which I will describe further on.

Knowing the routine and knowing about change is part of feeling safe

Routines, transitions, and change can be hugely challenging and frightening for some children and can often leave them feeling unsafe. Using visual timetables, personalised visual timetables, and now and next boards can all be helpful for the child to know what is happening during the day and what is happening next. There are some excellent examples in Kerry Murphy and Fifi Denham's book[60]. These are often routine parts of our whole group practice in early years, but some children need more than the class/group visual timetable; they may also need individual ones that adults can use with them. Also giving an individual additional warning before the change can help. Some children also need other visual prompts. I have one child who goes between mum and dad's house during the week; it is quite complicated as this happens on different days. The nursery and home now use visuals to show the child which parent is collecting and which house they are sleeping in. When the child asks the staff during the day, they can look at the visual together to remind them. We also need to remember that changes in routine, such as introducing dance in the afternoon instead of Yoga, visiting the park, and going on a trip, can all be unsettling and leave a child feeling unsafe. We can help children with this by preparing them beforehand, explaining what is going to happen, and showing them pictures. Thankfully, most of the schools I work in now use social stories routinely to support a bigger change, and this is so helpful that the staff usually writes it themselves. They are used for any school trips, nativity plays, visits, such as school nurses doing vaccinations, and many other changes. These are easy to write. I mentioned a link at the beginning of the book to Sheffield Hospital's explanation of social stories. There is also some useful information on the autism.org website[72]. Social stories are useful for many children, not just neurodivergent children.

Relationship with adults as part of feeling safe

For a long time in the UK, in the early years, we have used the key person approach, and I still think Peter Elfer and Elinor Goldschmeid's book[73] is very useful for embedding this approach. Children need to build attachments with key adults to help them feel safe. That move from home to nursery/childminder/school is massive and they can very easily feel unsafe and very sad. As I am writing this, it is mid-November 2023, and, as part of my work, my colleagues and I have been working with six nurseries in our area. We have noticed that this year's cohort of preschool children are increasingly finding the transition away from home incredibly difficult. Many of the children still cry a lot at the start of the day and through the day. It is taking the children a lot longer to settle and feel relaxed and safe. We are reminding ourselves, staff, and parents that this cohort is COVID-19 babies, and without a doubt, this has had a massive impact. Having strong relationships with staff is so important for the children to feel safe and be able to cope with that transition. I have heard some staff tell me that children build a strong relationship with one member of staff, their key person, but then when they are not in, it's a huge problem for the child. Using a buddy system can help, and having a second person/backup person to work alongside and get to know the child can also help with this issue.

CASE EXAMPLE

With one nursery, feeling safe was becoming a tricky issue for one child. He was a child in foster care, and he had made a firm attachment with his key person but was distraught if she wasn't in. When I visited the nursery, this was becoming a bigger difficulty as the child and family were moving house, so his anxiety was very high, and his window of tolerance was very small. It had reached the point that whenever the key person left the room, he was distraught. They had a backup person in place, but he was not happy with this setup. The staff were also concerned as the key person was due to go on leave for a week. They started to use a transitional object of the key person to give to the child when she stepped outside of the room; they used this for a few weeks, alongside physically handing him over to the other worker, placing his hand in her hand and saying, '*Lucy, please can you keep Luca safe while I go on my lunch.*' She also gave the little boy a small toy mouse of hers. She asked him to keep it safe for her while she was out of the room. It was small enough for him to hold or keep in his pocket. When she returned, the physical handover would happen again, and the mouse would be handed back. This took several days, but it began to make a difference. Then, when she was due to go on leave, on the last day, she told him she was going on holiday. She showed him photos of where she was going and how she would get there. They made a mini-calendar to count down when she would be back. She told him she would miss him and be thinking of him and gave him the mouse to take care of for her. She then handed him over again to the backup key person, asking her to keep him safe. She also pre-wrote a postcard for him (she was going abroad and it wouldn't have arrived in a week), this was given to him mid-week, and it told him she was thinking of him and looking forward to seeing him again. The week she was away wasn't all calm, but the things they put in place did help and provided him with some sense of safety.

Feeling that I belong

Knowing that you belong is a powerful feeling in the same way that having a sense that you don't belong is a strong feeling. Just for a moment, stop and think about a time you might have felt you didn't belong. How did that make you feel? When I first went to Nursery nursing college, I was 16, my mum had a severe mental illness, and I often needed to care for her. I hated school and did badly with my GCSE, but I wanted to work with children. I started college in a neighbouring city, and from day one, I felt like I did not belong. Many of the people in my course shared stories of nights out at clubs, getting drunk, and going to parties. My experience was so different; I went home to care for my mum and my sister. I felt different; back then, mental health wasn't talked about, and there was no recognition of young carers. Looking back now, I can see I was in a new world, and I felt out of my depth. Thankfully, things improved for me, not particularly at college. If I am honest, I always felt the odd one, but outside of college, I met a new set of friends where I felt like I belonged and felt welcomed. I left home at 17 and met the man I am now married to! If I look back and ask what might have helped me to feel I belong at college, one thing would have been having someone to talk to. Both adults and children need someone they can trust and speak to about the things that have been worrying and troubling them. Hopefully, children have this through their key person, and as adults, I hope we have the opportunity to talk through things that concern us with our supervisor.

Seeing ourselves represented

Another aspect of feeling that we belong is seeing ourselves and our family represented; this is so powerful. One of the children I am working with this year is a black boy who is in a class where all the other children are white. When I use stories which have black children in them, he points them out and comments they are like him. It is so important that our children don't just feel they are recognised and represented once a year during a black history celebration or celebrating a festival such as Diwali. If you want some advice on how to think about this and how to embed this in your practice, I would recommend reading Valerie Daniel's book[74]. As well as thinking about images we use, we also need to think about the toys we have and how children see themselves represented through the toys. Thankfully, toy makers are beginning to get better at this; with toys now representing colour and disabilities, we need to make sure we have a broad mix of these in our settings.

Knowing that people care for us

I think part of feeling that we belong is knowing that the people we are with are interested in us and care for us. We can show this through many different ways, and it is the same for children and staff. Some ways we can do this are:

Remembering birthdays and significant events such as moving house or passing exams
Having people check in with us if we look tired or have been unwell
Being offered some cake or chocolate (or fruit if that is your preference!)

Making suggestions of a book/film/exhibition we think they might like
Sharing food with one another; this might be eating together at lunchtime,
    making a meal for someone, or bringing in food we know they like.

Loving myself and feeling good about who I am

I have put these two areas together as I feel they are closely linked. I am
seeing a growing number of children who don't feel good about themselves.
They often make negative comments when they can't do something. My feeling
is that they don't love themselves, and they don't feel good about who
they are. I am going to suggest a few ways we can support children with this.

Recognise when the child is struggling and offer support

We all find things difficult and get things wrong, but some children (and
adults) can find the experience of getting things wrong or not managing to
achieve something really painful. I saw an example of that this week when
one little boy was sitting in phonics and was asked to write the word zigzag.
He threw his pen and whiteboard across the room and stormed off, shouting, 'I am not doing that. It's stupid.' He then sat in a corner, took his shoes
off, threw them, and looked very sad. Later, when we chatted about it,
I wondered if he was worried he couldn't do it or would get it wrong, and
he agreed. The feeling and the fear of getting it wrong was so huge that he
was overwhelmed by this. He felt and said he was stupid. I acknowledged
those feelings are really hard and can make us feel awful. I told him that
earlier, I had seen him writing the letter Z and saw it was hard for him, but
I was so impressed that he kept trying to manage it. He smiled at this. I told
him I found writing words hard and that I needed to keep practicing. I still
got things wrong with my words, but it was okay to get it wrong. We were
then able to move on and play with the things I had brought. I have no doubt
there will be many times this year when something similar happens, but my
hope is the staff and I can keep on reminding him we know he is finding it
hard, it is okay to find it hard, and we love it when he tries to do something
new and to celebrate when he tries something. Each child is different; some

children love to hear the words telling them that you are proud of them for trying something; other children like the non-verbal reaction, maybe a smile and thumbs up; other children like to have a small smile drawn on their work. We need to know how each individual child reacts and what works for them. This little boy loves to be told, but I know others who find that too hard, but a smile and a thumbs-up work for them.

Supporting children to feel okay to be noticed and praised

Some of the children my colleagues and I work with find it incredibly hard to be noticed. They visibly squirm when their name is called in the register and find it sometimes impossible to reply. They hate being noticed and praised and sometimes will rip up work if someone says it is good. One of my colleagues, Sharon, shared some lovely ways she supports children who find this hard. She focuses on their name to start with, making play dough with their name, writing their name in sand or flour, making biscuits and writing their name with icing pens on the biscuits. Doing lots of play around their name and using their name in this way helps them to become more comfortable with hearing it. Next, she tries to focus on something they are good at and be able to accept the praise 1–1 and then tell or show the teacher about the thing they have done. This can take time, and we need to build it up slowly at a pace the child is happy with. I had one child last year who found this very difficult and was unable to accept praise for a long time. We built it up by smiling, using a thumbs up, nodding, and then slowly introducing words such as '*I noticed how hard you tried then*,' or '*I loved how you did that*.' It was almost the end of the year until I could specifically praise him for something without him then destroying it.

Loving myself as an adult

For some, this is an incredibly hard area. We probably all know adults who find it hard to love themselves. This may be for many different reasons, including possible childhood traumas or unhappy current life experiences. In the section that follows, I take us through some practical ways to support our wellbeing, but if this is an area for you or a friend, I would suggest seeing if you can find a trained person to talk to for some therapy. This might be through contacting your GP and seeing if it is possible to get some talking therapy, or you might choose to go the private route and find a therapist to help you. For some people, it can be incredibly hard to love themselves, and they need some assistance in learning how to do this.

Being able to cope with life's difficulties

This links to the section on the window of tolerance and recognises that we all have different-sized windows of tolerance. For some children, their ability to cope with even what we might perceive as the smallest of difficulties can send them into a meltdown. It is essential that children have adults who are able to be calm and regulated to support them in dealing with difficulties. As mentioned previously, sometimes using tools such as visual timetables, pre-warnings of change, and social stories can all help with possible difficulties. But we can't always know what might be a trigger. I am currently working with one little boy, and many things trigger him, with his window of tolerance often being very small. This week, he became massively dysregulated at carpet time over a child saying something he wanted to say. He screamed and shouted and ran off. He has an incredible teaching assistant supporting him. She was calm, gave him some space, and sat near him but not too close to him (he doesn't like people in his space when he is dysregulated), but she was present. When he was ready, she gave him a hug, acknowledged how he was feeling, and asked if he was ready to come back. Later, she talked to him about other ways to manage that experience, but that needed to come later. A tool I often use with children who find it hard to share, take turns, and not be first is games. I have a wide selection of board games that I have bought over the years, mainly second-hand. They are games that are quick to play but work on the turn-taking, not being first. I love board games for teaching these skills; they are so useful. I often recommend to parents that they get some or ask for some from grandparents, aunts, and uncles for Christmas and birthday gifts. The Orchard games series[75] are great for this age; they all have similar types of rules, so once the child knows how to play one game, they have the skills for lots of them. Other favourites of the children I work with are Jenga, Pop Up Pirate, and Kerplunk (or the many different varieties of this).

How the adult can prioritise their and their colleague's wellbeing

I firmly believe we can only support a child's wellbeing when we have first looked after our own. Looking at our wellbeing is not a frivolous act. It is not selfish, and it doesn't need to cost money. Thankfully, staff and children's wellbeing have a lot more attention now, and a lot more is written about them. I wrote my first staff wellbeing book in 2017[54], and back then, it was a subject that was rarely talked about. However, with staff wellbeing, I sometimes become concerned when settings focus on one week a year wellbeing week. This can be lovely, but we need to ensure it is an embedded practice in our setting and for ourselves. In this section, I am going to share some ideas on how we can embed wellbeing into every day. This is both for ourselves and for our colleagues. This is about everyday wellbeing; I am not suggesting for a moment that this is about dealing with serious mental health illness. We need to be aware of the importance of seeking medical help when we are feeling mentally unwell. This might be through the GP or a charity such as Mind[76]. In what follows, I am going to explore a few wellbeing ideas:

Eat well
Sleep well
Spend time outside
Self-compassion
Do something that makes you happy
Experience some silence
Gratitude practice
Supporting colleagues

DOI: 10.4324/9781032692944-41

Eat well

We all know the advice around eating well, having at least five fruits and vegetables a day, and staying off food that is too sugary/too fatty/too salty. The research around food and the impact that it can have on our minds has hugely grown over the last few years. There is now a growing understanding that our gut health and our mental health are connected, and our gut microbiome plays an important part in our mental health (the gut microbiome is the bacteria in our guts). There is a growing amount of research in this area. One organisation called *Zoe*, led by Dr Tim Spector, is continuing to research this area and share information via their websites and podcasts[77]. One area that is suggested to improve our gut health is by eating a wide variety of mainly plant-based foods. This doesn't mean you have to be vegetarian or vegan, but it is a focus on plant-based food and avoiding, where possible, highly processed foods. Dr Tim Spector[78] suggests we all need to eat at least 30 different plant-based foods a week. This includes nuts, seeds, pulses, grains, fruit, vegetables, and herbs. When I first heard this figure, I wasn't convinced I and my family were doing this. I wrote down everything we ate for a few weeks, listing the plant-based foods (it's a bit of a pain but worth doing). We mostly cook from scratch, and I realised we were eating 30 plant-based foods by the middle of the week when you include things such as flour in bread, oats, coffee beans, chamomile tea, herbs, spices, beans and pulses, nuts, and seeds as well fruit and vegetables. I realised it wasn't as hard to reach as I first feared. I'm not saying that it's as easy as eating well and suddenly all your mental health and low wellbeing will be sorted, but I do think that reviewing and thinking about the food we eat can be helpful. As I am writing this, I am very aware that for many families, eating well can feel like a costly privilege. The cost of food over the last year in the UK has risen hugely, and we know that sometimes it is cheaper to buy a bulk bag of crisps than it is to buy a bag of fruit, and that is wrong. I know that cooking from scratch is not possible for some families. If they are unable to afford to use their hob/cooker, if they are juggling three jobs and have so little time at home, cooking from scratch can feel like, and be, one thing too many. I heard an amazing talk with Jack Munro, a food writer and anti-poverty campaigner, during the summer. She was speaking at Greenbelt

97

festival[79] about ways we can support everyone to eat healthily on a really small budget while reminding us that we need to campaign for the government to fully support families who are financially struggling.

Sleep well

Sleep is so important for our wellbeing. I know if I don't get enough sleep, I feel awful, I am bad-tempered, and I find it so hard to function. Guidance varies about how much sleep we need, and some say we shouldn't get too hung up on the numbers, but there seems to be a consensus in having around seven hours[80] of sleep a night for an adult. There can be many reasons why you might not get this. If you are a parent with a young baby/young child, if you are a peri-menopausal or menopausal, or if you are a carer, you may well find your sleep is impacted. If you are experiencing sleep difficulties due to peri-menopause or menopause, I recommend looking at the Balance[81] app/website run by Dr Louise Newson. It is agreed that regular lack of sleep can impact our cognition and our focus, can cause mood swings, and can contribute to a higher risk of serious illness. What follows are a few tips about sleep that you might find helpful:

- We can't catch up on sleep. The idea that we will catch up on sleep on the weekend or during a holiday is sadly a myth. The recommendation is to have a regular sleep pattern, going to bed and waking at a similar time each day
- Room temperature can impact our sleep. We don't want it too warm. The recommendation is around 18 Celsius, 65 Fahrenheit
- Darkness in the room helps you to sleep
- Having a warm bath or shower before bed may help you to sleep
- Alcohol and cigarettes are a stimulant and can keep you awake
- Having a warm drink before bed might help. I drink a sleepy herbal tea
- Using lavender on your pillow is sometimes helpful. I often make mini lavender pillows to go inside my pillowcase and give them as presents
- It is advised to turn off electric devices an hour before you go to bed. This means no phone scrolling! The light from the electronic device can make our brains believe it is daytime

- Reading a book before bed can be helpful
- Some people find a mindful meditation or similar can be useful. Many of the mindful apps have sleep meditations. I recommend Smiling Mind[82]; this is a free Australian mindfulness app with some excellent sleep meditations
- Some people find listening to music or calming sounds helpful. The composer Max Richter has written an 8.5-hour piece of work called *Sleep*. On his website, he describes it as 'a personal lullaby for a frenetic world'[83]. I love this piece of work; it is beautiful, and there is also a film about the music. You can find the music and the film on his website

For a while, I was concerned about how much sleep I was getting as I was aware that I was waking a lot due to the peri-menopause. During the same period, I got a new Fitbit[84] watch to track my swimming sessions, and I realised it had a sleep tracker on it. I find this useful and actually reassuring as it made me realise although I was waking a lot, I was still getting around 7.5 hours of sleep a night. But if sleep is an ongoing problem for you, it is worth speaking to your GP about it.

Spend time outside

As early years practitioners, we know that being outside can make a huge difference to children. They are often calmer, sometimes more engaged, and often happier. If it's good for children, it is no surprise that it is also good for us. It is believed that just ten minutes outside is enough to lower our stress levels. In Japan, there has been a huge amount of research on how being in nature can significantly lower our stress. They have a phrase called 'shinrin yoku'; in English, it can be translated as 'forest bathing.' When I first heard this phrase, I was so excited as I imagined pools of cool water in the forests; sadly, that isn't what they mean, but they have researched the impact being in forests or wooded areas has on the brain and stress levels. The idea of shinrin yoku is about walking slowly through trees, being in no hurry, noticing and appreciating what is around you, and bathing all your senses in the environment around you. Professor Yoshifumi Miyazaki from Chiba University has been studying how being in the woods can help us.

The research has shown that being in nature can reduce stress levels and boost our immune system. In Japan, this is now viewed as a preventable medicine and is prescribed by medics, and workplaces take their employees to the woods. Professor Yoshifumi has written a wonderful book describing his research and exploring in depth the benefits of shinrin yoku.[85]

You may not have woods near where you live, but we can still get the benefits of being outside, just by being outside the house or workplace. Thankfully, in the UK, we have many green spaces in our cities; maybe you can take a walk around your local park, spend time in a garden, or spend time in a nature area. If you live in a rural area, you might have fields around you. I live in a small village, and we have a community meadow at the bottom of our garden. I often walk around the meadow. It is small, and it is only a ten-minute walk if I walk slowly, but it has become a place I know will help me to destress. During lockdown, this was my sanctuary; I saw the sunrise every day from this space when I couldn't swim at the pool. I discovered we have a family of Tawny owls living in the trees. When you have time outside, think about turning off your devices. We are often tempted to listen to music or maybe a podcast, but if we can fully be in nature, hearing the sounds of birds, noticing the smells around us, and touching the trees or plants, this will help to lower our stress hormones. Some GPs are now prescribing time in nature for some of their patients[86].

What follows are some ideas on how to bring some more nature into your life.

Grow some food or flowers. You don't need a garden for this; you can grow food such as salad leaves, herbs, tomatoes, and beans in pots. Many flowers are happy to grow in pots, such as marigolds, calendula, violas, sweetpeas, and small roses. Seeds are cheap to buy; you don't need expensive ones, and supermarket seeds are fine. I have a garden which I love, and I also often plant bulbs in the winter to grow inside. There is something wonderful about the early colour and joy of hyacinth flowers and daffodils.

Forage. You need to be careful about this and know what you are picking. There are many websites and books that can guide you. The obvious fruit to forage most people know is blackberry. There is something very wonderful about picking free food to eat. I love foraging and take such joy from finding wild garlic in the early spring. It always feels like a sign of hope that winter is ending. The Woodland Trust has a helpful posting on its website about the foods you can forage throughout the year.[87]

Bring the outside in. This could be by buying some flowers, growing bulbs, bringing in holly, or even just a collection of conkers. By bringing the outside into your house, you are increasing those moments of connection with nature. I am currently writing this book in November. It is becoming dark around 5 p.m., and there have been many days of rain. I have recently bought two cheap Amaryllis bulbs. They are growing in my dining room and living room; one of them is currently in flower; they have big flowers, which are a delight to see. The flowers will last for weeks; they are so simple, but provide me with a moment of joy each time I look at them.

Figure 3.1

Find places near you where you can spend time in nature. You probably know where your local green areas are, but there may be some little gems you were not aware of, maybe a local allotment area that you can walk through, a hidden graveyard (this may sound odd, but these can be great mini sanctuaries of nature) or wildlife area. It is worth doing a little bit of research, looking at Google Maps or Googling 'nature areas near me,' and asking local friends and family where they connect with nature. Doing a little bit of research and planning and then pencilling in a time when you can go and visit a new spot of nature can be a great small boost.

Exercise outside. This can be an excellent way of connecting with nature through quick walking, going for a run, wild swimming, or using a park exercise trail. I swim daily in a local pool, but my joy is in outdoor swimming. I love the combination of being outside in nature and in water, and if it's cold water, even better. I have learnt that outdoor swimming is always an immediate stress release for me. I love swimming in the sea, in the rivers, or even in a lido. If you are interested in wild swimming (swimming that is not in an indoor pool), do some research first, read guidance around wild swimming[88], and don't swim alone.

Self-compassion

I think self-compassion is one of the most powerful skills we can learn in supporting our wellbeing. Self-compassion is about how we treat ourselves kindly, how we speak to ourselves kindly, and how we are loving to ourselves. For a long time, I had a critical inner voice. If I did something wrong, it would run through my mind over and over again; this is often referred to as ruminating. Through the ruminating, I would often berate myself over what I did or said. I suspect I am not unusual in this. I started a mindfulness course, and this helped to slow down or stop the ruminating. In a later section, I am going to talk about mindfulness. The writer and person who helped me to think about self-compassion was Kristin Neff. I first heard a great TED talk[89] from her and then read her first book called *Self-Compassion*[45]. I found her work incredibly inspiring. Her message is that we need to learn to speak to ourselves in the way we would speak to a special friend. She suggests that often, our inner voice can be cruel, unkind, and harsh, saying words to ourselves that we would never say to anyone else. She suggests that we can create an inner script where we change the words we speak, offering some gentleness and kindness, some love. If you have spent years being self-critical, this is incredibly hard to change, but it is worth trying. I have found it has made a massive difference; occasionally, I slip back into the negative voice, but mostly I have learnt to stop it and be kinder. Her book has many helpful tips and suggestions on how to start becoming more compassionate to ourselves.

One part of being self-compassionate is understanding how we are feeling and how we are responding to situations. Having the ability to reflect on what we feel and how we respond is so useful; along with this, having the understanding and the words for our complex emotions and feelings. Brene Brown's book *Atlas of the Heart*[20] offers an exploration of 87 emotions and feelings. Once we have the name and understanding of how we are feeling, we are in a better place to understand what we are experiencing and to respond kindly.

One very simple self-compassion exercise that I regularly suggest to people is a hand massage. Just for a moment, I encourage you to go and find some hand cream, then take a moment to gently and slowly massage it into your hands. This very simple act is an act of self-compassion. You are taking a moment to show yourself some self-love and self-care. I regularly recommend to staff I work with that they have some hand cream in their classroom/nursery room so they can take a moment to show themselves some self-care.

Do something that makes you happy

This might sound incredibly frivolous, but as I mentioned in the first section, we want to build joyful memories into our memory so we can call on these when life is difficult. I know that when life, work, and the outside world feel hard and depressing, it can feel like one thing too many to think about doing something that makes us happy. We often end up in survival mode and coping mode. However, I do believe that if we can bring in small practices of moments that make us happy, this really can support our wellbeing. This doesn't have to be big, expensive gestures; it can be simple, small moments of happiness. It might be listening to some music and having a dance in the kitchen while you make tea, having a hot bath with a glass of wine on a Friday evening, going for a walk with a friend or a loved one, or baking a cake and enjoying eating a slice with a cup of coffee. I often find December a hard month; work in schools is crazy in the run-up to Christmas, and the juggle of finishing work, meeting extended family Christmas expectations, and the shorter days all lead to me often feeling exhausted. This year, I decided to make myself a virtual advent calendar of joyful moments. There is a website you can use to create one for free[90]. Each day, I have put a photo and a suggestion of something I can do that will make me happy. I'm hoping it will be a lovely small reminder each day and will help me through the month. Examples are small things such as going for a walk, watching the birds, having a glass of wine in the bath, and, of course, a reminder to do a cold water swim!

Experience some silence

I have noticed that life feels noisier. As someone who spends a lot of time in reception classes and nurseries, they are often incredibly loud places. As the term goes on, I often crave more times of quiet. Just for a moment, stop and think about when you last had some time of silence. Some people find silence intimidating and will do anything to fill it. I believe if we can learn to sit with silence it can be so helpful to our wellbeing. We know that in conversations, it is sometimes the silent moments that can be the most powerful. In my role as a nurture worker with children, I have learnt that we need to be able to sit with the silence. It is the moments of silence that sometimes children can find their voice to tell us what they need us to hear.

Some people question if too much noise in our lives can contribute to depression and mental health difficulties. There are different ways we can introduce some silence in our lives. I am not suggesting we all need to go on a silent retreat, although I have friends who have done these, and they have found them incredibly beneficial. It could be you have some time in the house without the radio or TV on, although you may live in a busy household with noisy family members where the lack of the TV or radio makes little difference. Or it might be that if you go for a walk, have some time where you don't listen to music or a podcast, enabling you to hear the sounds around you of bird songs or the wind through the trees.

Mindfulness or yoga can also be a useful way to engage in times of more quietness. It won't be total silence, although there are moments of silence within these practices. Both of these practices can be useful in some times of silence. For mindfulness, you could use an app; I recommend Smiling Mind app[86], which is a free app and has a range of meditations from five minutes to longer ones. It is a great tool if you are starting out with mindfulness. For yoga, there are many lessons you can attend in the community, or you can do yoga lessons online. I recommend Yoga with Adriene[91], which is free.

Gratitude practice

Several years ago, I heard some information about gratitude practice from Brene Brown[92]. She was talking about her research that found a link between people who were joyful about their lives and a gratitude practice. The research showed that having a daily gratitude practice invited joyfulness into your life. Several faiths encourage this practice, but also many people who don't engage in faith have this regular practice. I try to use this practice daily before I go to sleep. I think through the day and name three things I am grateful for; sometimes, it is as simple as the coffee I drank in the morning, the red kite I saw on my journey home, and my husband cooked tea that evening. Other times, it might be about work or something I read, saw, or watched. It doesn't matter what the things that I am grateful for are; for me, it's about remembering that each day, there have been moments that were good. In my role and sometimes in the darkness of the world news around us, it can feel that everything is dark. In the past, I have easily entered into a spiral of feeling that everything is bad, but I have found this daily gratitude practice has helped me to shift my thinking.

Another advocate of gratitude practice is Dr Julie Smith[93]. In her book, she suggests a gratitude practice can be a useful part of our self-care toolkit. She recommends that a daily practice of writing down three things we are grateful for can help to reframe what our mind focuses on. When we think about the things we are grateful for and allow ourselves a few moments to notice how they make us feel, this can help to develop new pathways in our brain.

Supporting colleagues

Many of us spend a lot of time with our colleagues, and our colleague's wellbeing can impact our wellbeing. There are workplaces I have been in where the general mood and wellbeing of most of the staff is really low. One or two staff having a low time can have an impact on the whole team. I am not writing this as a critical view but as a recognition that we can all have an impact on one another. As mentioned under the mental health first aid section, Kate Moxley[38] has written an excellent book, *A guide to mental health for early years educators*, that is worth looking at for ideas on how to recognise when your colleague may be struggling with their mental health and how you can support them.

There is growing recognition that being kind to others and showing acts of kindness to others supports them but also boosts our wellbeing. Doing something or being kind to someone else can help to build a sense of belonging and lessen feelings of isolation; it can also help to keep things in perspective. There are various websites which can offer ideas and suggestions on how to be kind to others. *The Guardian* has a list of 52 things you could do through the year[94]. There is a website for random acts of kindness[95] which offers ideas for home, school, and the workplace. I offer a few ideas based on things I have experienced and what we do in our team:

- Bake a cake for your team meeting
- Bring flowers into the office
- Remember colleagues' birthdays
- Celebrate achievements e.g. gaining a qualification
- Thank colleagues for their work
- Tell colleagues when you are impressed by their work
- Buy chocolate to share!
- Make a cup of tea/coffee for a colleague
- Cover someone so they can have a coffee break
- Have hand cream in the room so colleagues can take a moment for a hand massage
- Make jam/chutneys for your colleagues
- Share produce from your garden
- Check in with colleagues and ask how they are
- Remember important times for colleagues and offer extra support, for example, if a child is leaving home/bereavement/moving house.

All of these ideas on supporting your wellbeing are very simple. There is nothing groundbreaking or radical about them; however, taking the time, a few moments of intention to look after ourselves, can make a difference.

How we can create an enabling environment which promotes wellbeing

There are many ways we can ensure our environment promotes the wellbeing of children and staff. I am going to offer a few ideas and suggestions on how we can think about this:

- **What do people think?**
- **The space**
- **The ethos**
- **Am I welcome?**

What do people think?

I think this is a good place to start, to find out what your staff, children, and parents think about how you promote wellbeing. I have been in plenty of settings where the managers think they have created an environment that promotes wellbeing, but where it is evident as an outsider, that is not the case. It takes openness to answer this question. If you are a manager reading this, do you really know what your staff, children, and parents think about how you promote wellbeing in your setting? It is only worth exploring this if you are genuinely interested and willing to listen. A few ways you could find out are:

Survey/questionnaire

Do a mini survey with staff and parents/carers, asking open-ended questions about how they feel wellbeing is supported in your setting. Ask for suggestions of other things that could be implemented.

DOI: 10.4324/9781032692944-42

Photo journey

With the children, you could talk to them about feeling loved, welcomed, being looked after, and how they belong in your setting. You could ask them for examples of how they see/experience this. You could then ask them to take some photos of things in the setting that make them feel loved, welcomed, and that they belong. I often get children to take photos using the iPad. They are usually familiar with the technology and are often confident taking photos on an iPad. You could also ask staff and parents/carers to take photos of examples of wellbeing in the setting. It would be interesting to compare these and see the different ideas. You could put all the photos up on a display for all to see.

Planning forward

Once you have heard/seen the views of all involved in the setting, you might then like to make a plan or list of ideas and ways forward, new things to implement, or things to change. Make sure you also have your voice heard within this process; as a manager, you have a responsibility to support the wellbeing in the setting but also don't ignore your wellbeing.

The space

The physical space has an impact on our wellbeing. What follows are a few things to consider:

Do you have a dedicated staff room that is free of clutter and child-free?
Is there a quiet space for children to enjoy
Is the environment warm in the winter and cool in the summer?
Do you have windows you can open?
Does the environment have natural light?
How noisy is the environment?
How does the environment smell?
Do you have easy access outside?

Do you have examples of the natural world inside?

Do all the staff and children have a space to put their belongings?

Is there water/drinks available at all times for everyone?

Is there food available for children and staff?

Are the toilets clean and uncluttered, and do they have sanitary products available for staff?

Are there signposts for staff and parents in the form of leaflets/posters for mental health support/Domestic Violence/menopause advice?

These are just a few ideas and quite varied, but they make a difference. It may not be possible to do all of these. I know in some settings, such as pack-away preschools, it can be out of your control to have a space for a staff room or be able to open windows. However, there are some things, such as access to drinks/water, which are possible for everyone and are extremely basic but so important. I also believe touches such as sanitary products and providing tea/coffee for staff are small ways to show you care. I do understand there is a cost involved, and this can be hard, particularly in these current financial times.

The ethos

This is about the culture of the setting, the values, and the culture you create. Managers will often lead on this, but all staff have a part to play in this. In my role, I work in many different schools and nurseries, and I can often tell if a setting has a strong ethos of wellbeing within minutes of being there. That may sound slightly crazy, but I do believe that when a place has an embedded ethos of wellbeing, you will know almost immediately. As you walk through the doors, it can begin to feel apparent. This isn't just in schools and nurseries; a member of our team this week shared how she recently moved her mum into a supported living place. She described how, as you walk through the doors, you are welcomed by photos and names of the staff. You then see another board that tells you who is in today, who has made the food today, and who is cleaning today, again with photos. She described how all staff know everyone's names, both the residents and their families, and how everyone is made to feel welcomed and is spoken to as they walk through the building. Since moving, Kate's Mum has begun to thrive again, and Kate is feeling calmer knowing her mum is being cared for and loved. When Kate described this to the team, we talked about how this is the same for the little ones we support. I can think of a few schools where I have an extremely frosty welcome from the staff when I arrive in the reception area. They don't seem to remember my name, and if they do, they don't use it; they barely look up and often roll their eyes if I request something, such as if they can open the locked door for me. In contrast, there are other schools where all the staff seem to know me and all staff say hello, ask how I am, some ask what exciting things am I doing today, others know I swim and might ask if I have been in cold water that week. I have noticed that if staff take time to speak to and be kind to visitors, not in a false quick way, but in a real way, then they often show a kindness and nurturing approach to their staff, parents, and children.

Having an embedded ethos of wellbeing in a setting is not just having a week in the year when we provide a few nice gifts to staff and offer yoga to staff and children; embedding wellbeing is about ensuring every day we care for all. Part of a wellbeing ethos is that everyone feels that we are interested in them, that we love them, and care for them. Yes, we expect our staff to work at their allotted tasks; yes, we expect everyone to do their job to the best of their ability; and yes, we expect staff to be honest and trustworthy. We also want everyone to care for one another, to be kind to one another, and to be interested and welcoming to each other. An interesting exercise to do as a team is to write a statement together about your ethos and values. In the team I work for, we have recently been through some changes, and we are looking at this again for ourselves. It is an inspiring and interesting exercise to do, and one you want to take time over, but to do it well, I would say it takes courage and honesty. It is easy to write grand statements, but do you believe them, live them, and embed them?

Am I welcome?

As I mentioned previously, there are settings I work in where I know I am welcomed, but in the same way, there are one or two other settings where I don't feel welcomed. How do we welcome everyone? If you have reception staff in your setting, this is a good place to start! I am sure we have all experienced a frosty receptionist in a doctor's/school's/dentist's, and it doesn't feel good. Over the years, I have delivered a lot of listening to young children training for children's centre staff, particularly when we used to have a lot of children's centres in the UK. Whenever I deliver the training, I ask for all staff to attend, including the reception and admin staff. The reason for this is that the first person a child and their family will encounter as they arrive at a children's centre is the admin/receptionist staff, and their welcome can make or break the start of the session. I think their role is a powerful one in helping people to feel welcome or not.

We want everyone entering our setting to feel that they are welcomed and they belong; part of this is by seeing ourselves represented. Ideally, this would be done by seeing other people in the setting who look like us, but this can also be done through the books, toys, images, and words we have around. One of my previous books is a conversation with early years practitioner Jamel Carly-Campbell[96]. In this book, we have conversations about how we embed a culture of welcome, belonging, and working with one another. Jamel is a black male working in London, and I am a white, middle-aged woman working in Somerset. We have totally different backgrounds and experiences, but through this book, we share ideas of how to embed a culture of welcome. I loved hearing his thoughts on this; a big takeaway for me was how he talked about linking to the community you are based in, forging good connections and relationships with the community, taking part with them in cultural and local events, and inviting the local community in.

How we can engage parents and work in partnership with them when supporting their children's wellbeing

I think this is a really important area to think about. Since the COVID-19 pandemic, we are seeing a greater number of young children with high anxiety. COVID seems to have played a part in that; the vital lack of socialising outside of their family at a young age has played its part, but I also think a higher number of parents are anxious, and I wonder if this is also contributing to anxious children. We are increasingly thinking about how we can support our staff's wellbeing and children's wellbeing, but I think we also need to ask the question of how we can support parents' wellbeing and help them to have an understanding of how they can support their children's wellbeing. I am going to offer a few areas to think about in this section.

Information sharing about wellbeing for children and themselves

Just for a moment, think about how you help parents learn about supporting the wellbeing of their children. Some settings will specifically talk about this in their newsletters/online updates/parents' evenings. Other settings have notice boards sharing wellbeing ideas. In one nursery I work with, we send home some parent and child activities that will support the child's wellbeing – simple suggestions that help the parent and child connect with one another. For example, sending home a play dough recipe and suggesting they make playdough together, or sending home a suggestion for going on a nature walk in the spring and noticing how many different coloured plants they can see. We send one a week with no pressure or expectation but an invitation for them to use it if they think it would be helpful. I know another nursery that holds a

112

parent's evening three times a year and shares wellbeing ideas with the parents. Sometimes, this is aimed at ways to support their children, and sometimes, it is ideas for how the parents can support their own wellbeing. Other settings have a lending library of books they can share with parents, with a mix of books to support parents and parenting and also wellbeing books for children. I have recommended many different books that could be included in a library in the further suggestions part after Section 1 of this book. In the way we want to be able to encourage and nurture the wellbeing of our staff and children, we also want the parents to be a crucial part of this, and if we can help them with this by offering a few ideas, equipping them, signposting them, this will be so beneficial to the families.

Open conversations

I know that often, the drop-off and pick-up time can be busy and fraught, with parents wanting to leave to get to work and children keen to get home. However, we want to make sure that parents and carers have the opportunity to tell us about things which might be or are impacting the family. As early years professionals, we all know that even if a child doesn't know about a change, for example, a parent being ill, they can sense it, and they will react to it. The drop-off and pick up time is not always the best time to inform you, so it is worth looking at what other systems you have in place. This might be through a web-based feedback system, or it might be as simple as a notebook between home and the setting. We often use the notebook system with several of the children I work with in schools. The parents are able to write down things such as if it has been a bad night or if the child was unable to have breakfast that morning. The staff looks at the book as the child arrives and immediately knows if they need to adapt things for the child. I think it can be helpful in our policies and information to parents to remind them to let us know if there are things that might be impacting their child and family and to explain why it is helpful for us to know and how even a baby can pick up on stress in the family. We are able to help the child so much more when we know what is happening. I know that for some families, this can be extremely hard; they may feel their problems are a private matter and not one to be discussed, but I think if we can help families understand that we are all there for the wellbeing of the child, and if as a setting we understand a little of what might be happening for the child, we are in a better place to support them.

Signposting

There was a time when there was a lot more funding in the early years in the UK when Sure Start was in place under the Labour government. At this time, many nurseries and schools were able to refer families to children's centres for additional support and information. It was a system that was accessible to all. Sadly, things have changed, and a lot of early help that was available is not available anymore, although I am hopeful this will change again. However, what this means, for now, is that we all need to be better about knowing what is available in our local area to be able to signpost families. I think it can be so useful to have a list of the local projects in your area, so if a family is in need, you can immediately signpost them and share some details about how they can get help. It takes a little bit of time to pull together, but if you can find the time for someone in your setting to do this, it is so beneficial. You might want a file with info so you can quickly turn it in, although check periodically that it is up to date. You might also want posters around to signpost parents. Here are a few areas to think about:

- Food bank – Find out how families can access the food bank in your area and eligibility for this
- Food pantry – This is different from a food bank, often run by different organisations and has different criteria; more people are eligible for a food pantry
- Clothing/baby bank – More areas now have these. They are often run by a charity, and usually, a nursery or health visitor can refer
- Domestic violence support – There will be a local team or charity in your area offering support for DV
- Drug and alcohol addiction – There will be a local team or charity in your area offering support for drug and alcohol addiction
- Health visitor team – Over the last few years, there have been many changes to health visitors. I have noticed that a lot of the families I see

don't have a specific named health visitor anymore. Find out how families access health visitors in your area

- Special education team – There will be a SEND team in your area, often with parent support advisors as part of them. It is very useful to know how families can access this support if they need it
- Mind – This is a national charity with 100 local Mind centres. It is worth finding out if you have a local centre in your area and how adults can access their support. Their website[97] tells you where the centres are located
- Bereavement information – There will be charities in your area that offer bereavement support; it might be worth finding out which ones are local to you. Cruse[98] has 80 branches, and their website can direct you to where these are. The bereavement advice website[99] is also a useful website with information about national charities, how to register a death and inform others, the funeral, probate, money, and tax; these are all areas that can be so baffling and overwhelming for a family, having a note of the website that you can share with a family might be the small moment of help they need

How to write a wellbeing policy

Every early years setting and school should have a staff wellbeing policy. I know that by having a policy, you are not guaranteed to have a good wellbeing ethos in your setting, but it is a good start; it sets out a clear intention for everyone to see and understand. Ideally, your wellbeing policy would be written together with your team. If you already have a wellbeing policy and it hasn't been reviewed for a while, I recommend that you review it together as a team and be honest about whether it is still the policy you all want to have. If you haven't got a staff wellbeing policy in place, now is the perfect time to start this process.

Staff wellbeing survey

If having a staff wellbeing policy is a new venture for you, start by talking to staff about it and give them some time to think about it. You might want to start the process by conducting a confidential staff survey to find out how people are feeling. There is an excellent example of a staff survey on the CORC[100] (Child Outcomes Research Consortium) website, they worked in collaboration with the Anna Freud Centre on this. If you do a staff survey, it is so important that staff feel and know that it is safe for them to be honest. Doing a staff survey helps you to know how your staff is feeling, how they are experiencing their job, what might be impacting their mental health both at work and outside of work, whether they feel equipped to support their own wellbeing and the children's wellbeing, and if they feel supported. It is recommended that you routinely do staff wellbeing surveys at least once a year. There are limitations to a staff survey; it is only a glimpse into people's thoughts, but I think it can be a valuable starting point. I do

DOI: 10.4324/9781032692944-44

acknowledge that it can be hard to keep them anonymous when you are in a small staff team, even without people's names on them. As a manager, you may realise who has filled them in, and it might be obvious if you share the data. As a manager, you have a responsibility to help staff know you will keep them safe when filling this out. Have an honest conversation as a team before doing a staff survey, and find out their thoughts first. If your team is not convinced, then you might want to rethink, as forcing them to do a staff wellbeing survey will not support their wellbeing.

If you have done a staff survey, this could help you to establish some areas of need be in your setting, and this will change over time. I know that sometimes a particular cohort of children can have a massive impact on the wellbeing of staff. If the children have high SEMH needs, social care needs, or SEN needs, all of these things can impact staff. It is so important managers and staff are mindful of this. This is also the reason why we need to ensure that talking about staff wellbeing is not just a once-a-year event during the staff survey or while reviewing policies. It needs to be something we consider all year.

Writing the policy

Ideally, writing the policy will be a joint venture with managers and all staff. Everyone in the setting has a role to play in this and should have a voice in the process. If you have done a staff survey, you could share the results from this in an anonymised way, reflect on these results, and think about how these can be used within your policy. On the Anna Freud website[101], there is a useful booklet with guidance on how to write a staff wellbeing policy; this is linked to a survey they did in collaboration with the National Day Nurseries Association and a few local authorities. Your policy needs to be unique to your setting; however, their booklet offers some ideas on what you can include. It has some suggestions for headings which may be useful. These include:

- Why is this policy important?
- What are the values of your settings that underpin this policy?
- What is the aim of your policy?

- What are your objectives?
- How will you achieve them? What actions will you take?
- How will you review this policy?

Implementing the policy

Your wellbeing policy needs to be a living and working document, not a piece of paper you write once and put in a file to be reviewed in a year. Once you have written it and everyone has agreed to the policy, you want to think about how you make sure you are all involved in implementing it. This could vary from ensuring staff wellbeing is on the agenda for everyone's supervision, having a staff wellbeing slot on the team agenda – this might be a time when people take turns to share some tips and ideas – or when you discuss how things are working and what needs changing. You may want to look at the information you have available in your setting regarding signposting; for example, I noticed in one Infants school I work in that the staff toilets have information about menopause support on their doors. You might want different members of staff to take the lead on certain areas, for example, having a rotation to make sure there is tea/coffee/drinks available. I know one nursery that has a rotation for bringing in cake. You might want a rotation through the year if different members of staff are looking for new information on wellbeing or mental health, either in books or online. New ideas that are easily found continue to be offered and updated. In the next section, I offer some suggestions of places to look. As a team, I am sure you will have many ideas on how you can make sure this stays a live and relevant policy. It is also important that any new staff arriving know about the wellbeing policy and have the opportunity to talk about it and, of course, read it. If I were joining a new team, I would feel encouraged if staff wellbeing was mentioned right at the start of the recruitment process. You may decide as part of the policy that you want staff trained in mental health first aid; as mentioned in the first section, Kate Moxley[102] is a mental health first aid trainer with a background in early years.

Signposting for further advice

Thankfully, the importance of embedding wellbeing practice into our own lives and embedding it in our practice and settings is now far more recognised. Over the last few years, the number of organisations where it is possible to get advice in this area has been growing. The following are a few places I recommend looking at:

- ACAS is a useful organisation to find out about your rights as a worker and your responsibilities as an employer. They have useful information on how to manage employees' wellbeing in the workplace[103]
- Mind is a mental health charity and has a page on its website with advice on mental health at work[104]. They also have a page with free resources on how to take care of staff's mental health in the workplace[105]
- Anna Freud is a mental health charity for children and families. They have a lot of information regarding the mental health and wellbeing of staff and children. In previous sections, I have referred to their specific booklets on embedding wellbeing, but the whole website is worth looking at for further ideas[106]
- Gov.UK – The UK Government has a web page dedicated to early years practitioner wellbeing with links to organisations and some case studies to look at[107]
- Every Mind Matters is an NHS website with ideas and suggestions on how to support your wellbeing. They have a short and simple quiz you can do, and they offer suggestions based on your answers. You can also sign up for anxiety-easing emails, where they email you suggestions around easing anxiety, or you may want to get their sleep tips emailed to you. This is a useful resource and

DOI: 10.4324/9781032692944-45

worth having a poster or information about it for all staff and parents to know about[108]

- Hub of Hope is a mental health database. You can put in your postcode and the area you want support with, and they will tell you of organisations in your area that can provide support. This is a mix of community, peer, charity, private, and NHS support in your area. The subjects you can ask for support are varied; some examples are mental health conditions, disability, ex-forces, perinatal support, rural and agricultural support, student support, and many others. I think this is a brilliant resource and was a new discovery for me as I was doing the research for this book[109]

Staff training

We all know that staff training is vital for all staff. There are many ways you can include wellbeing in your CPD agenda. I think a good approach is to have a mix of ways your staff can access staff wellbeing information. You may include regular small staff wellbeing information sharing as part of your team meetings. Your local authority may provide wellbeing hubs where staff can attend a regular session based on a wellbeing subject. The local authority where I am based, Bath and North East Somerset, provide these throughout the year, and I deliver them. Some charities run mental health training, such as Mind[110], and as I have mentioned previously, you could get staff trained in mental health first aid[111].

Anna Freud's website[112] has training you can attend online. Early Education[113] delivers courses, some of these are on wellbeing. Kathy Brodie[114] regularly has speakers on her Early Years TV covering the subject of wellbeing. There are also a number of platforms, such as Kinderly[115], Parenta[116], and Famly[117], that all offer training, and some of these will be on the subject of wellbeing.

Another option is organising an outside trainer or speaker for your staff meetings or putting on an event with other local nurseries and bringing in an outside trainer to talk about staff wellbeing. This is something I regularly do[118], and other early years trainers will also do.

DOI: 10.4324/9781032692944-46

Conclusion

I hope this book has offered you a little more insight and understanding into wellbeing. I often describe my books and training as a menu approach. There will be things in the menu that are attractive to you that you would like to try, and there will be other things on the menu that are not for you today, and that is fine. I hope you were able to find the thing that you needed today from reading this book. Thank you for taking the time to read it, whether it was a dip in and out or read it all the way through approach; I appreciate you spending your precious time with it.

I hope that, after your time with this book, you can now step away and do something for your wellbeing. I am just finishing this book as we approach Christmas 2023, and today it is the solstice. I went for a cold water swim this morning in the recently reopened lido that has opened in Bath, and this evening, I plan on making some mulled cider, celebrating finishing this book, and welcoming in Christmas and the start of the longer days. I hope you can find something nurturing to do for your wellbeing.

DOI: 10.4324/9781032692944-47

References

Section 1

1. NHS-generalised anxiety disorder. https://www.nhs.uk/mental-health/conditions/generalised-anxiety-disorder/overview/
2. NHS Managing anxiety. https://www.nhs.uk/every-mind-matters/mental-health-issues/anxiety/
3. Sheffield children's NHS social stories. https://library.sheffield childrens.nhs.uk/social-stories/
4. Felitti, V., Anda, R., Nordenberg, D., Williamson, D., Spitz, A., Edwards, V., Koss, M., & Marks, J. (1998) Relationship of childhood abuse and household dysfunction to many of the leading causes of death in adults: The Adverse Childhood Experiences (ACE) Study. *American Journal of Preventive Medicine*, 14(4), 245–258. https://pubmed.ncbi.nlm.nih.gov/9635069/
5. Burke-Harris, N. (2018) *The deepest well. Healing the long term effects of childhood adversity.* London: Bluebird.
6. ACEs film. www.youtube.com/watch?v=XHgLYI9KZ-A
7. Anna Freud attachment. https://www.annafreud.org/early-years/early-years-in-mind/resources/what-is-attachment/
8. Siegel, D. & Payne-Bryson, T. (2020) *The power of showing up.* London: Scribe.
9. Reggio Emilia approach. https://www.reggiochildren.it/en/reggio-emilia-approach/
10. Mainstone-Cotton, S. (2023) *Creativity and wellbeing in early the years.* Abingdon: Routledge.

11. NHS description. https://www.nhs.uk/mental-health/conditions/depression/
12. Mind web page on depression. https://www.mind.org.uk/information-support/types-of-mental-health-problems/depression/about-depression/
13. NHS link for children with depression. https://www.nhs.uk/mental-health/children-and-young-adults/advice-for-parents/children-depressed-signs/
14. Grimmer, T. (2022) *Supporting behaviour and emotions in the early years; strategies and ideas for early years educators.* Abingdon: Routledge.
15. Delahooke, M. (2020) *Beyond behaviours using brain science and compassion to understand and solve children's behavioural challenges.* London: John Murray Press.
16. Delahooke, M. (2022) *Brain body parenting: How to stop managing behaviour and start managing joyful, resilient kids.* London: John Murray Press.
17. Early intervention foundation. https://www.eif.org.uk/what-its-about/early-years
18. Buckler, R. (2023) *Developing child centred practice for safeguarding and child protection.* Abingdon: Routledge.
19. Mona Delahooke. https://monadelahooke.com/emotional-regulation-springboard-childrens-mental-health/
20. Brown, B. (2021) *Atlas of the heart.* London: Vermilion (p. 204).
21. Llenas, A. (2016) *The colour monster.* London: Templar Publishing.
22. Jarman, E. (2013) *The communication friendly spaces approach.* Camber: Elizabeth Jarman Limited.
23. Garvey, D. (2023) *Little brains matter.* Abingdon: Routledge.
24. Parenta. https://www.parenta.com/wp-content/uploads/2021/07/The-importance-of-holistic-development-in-early-years-final.pdf
25. Birth to five matters. https://birthto5matters.org.uk/
26. Payne, K. (2022) *Supporting the wellbeing of children with SEND.* Abingdon: Routledge.
27. Daniel, V. (2023) *Anti-racist practice in the early years.* Abingdon: Routledge.

28. Clark, A. & Moss, P. (2011) *Listening to young children: The mosaic approach.* London: National Children's Bureau.

29. Mainstone-Cotton, S. (2019) *Listening to young children in early years settings.* London: Jessica Kingsley Publishers.

30. Page, J. (2011) Do mothers want professional carers to love their babies? *Journal of Early Childhood Research,* 9(3), 310–323. https:// journals.sagepub.com/doi/pdf/10.1177/1476718X11407980

31. Professional love in early years settings a report of the summary findings. https://eymatters.co.uk/wp-content/uploads/2020/05/pleys-report_ singlepages.pdf

32. Grimmer, T. (2021) *Developing a loving pedagogy in early years.* Abingdon: Routledge.

33. Grimmer, T. (forthcoming 2024) *Loving pedagogy explained.* Abingdon: Routledge.

34. Leicestershire wellbeing and involvement. https://resources.leicestershire. gov.uk/education-and-children/early-years/childcare-practice/personal- development-behaviour-and-welfare/well-being-and-involvement

35. Woman's hour. https://www.bbc.co.uk/programmes/articles/2nRkccX R7FfQvD53H3D4zzp/brene-brown-seven-things-we-learned-about- our-emotions-from-the-best-selling-author-on-woman-s-hour

36. Mental health first aid England. https://mhfaengland.org/individuals/ adult/

37. Moxley, K. (2022) *A guide to mental health for early years educators.* Abingdon: Routledge.

38. Louv, R. (2005) *Last child in the woods saving our children from nature deficit disorder.* Chapel Hill, NC: Algonquin Books.

39. Mcfarlane, R. & Morris, J. (2017) *The lost words.* London: Penguin.

40. Oxford learner dictionary. https://www.oxfordlearnersdictionaries. com/definition/english/nurture_1

41. Mainstone-Cotton, S. (2021) *Supporting children with social, emotional and mental health needs in the early years.* Abingdon: Routledge

42. Watkins, S. (2022) *Outdoor play for healthy little minds.* Abingdon: Routledge.

43. Mainstone-Cotton, S. (2017) *Promoting emotional wellbeing in early years staff.* London: Jessica Kingsley Publishers.

44. Neff, K. (2011) *Self compassion*. London: Hodder & Stoughton.
45. Byers, G. (2020) *I am enough*. New York: Balzer and Bray.
46. NHS Self-harm. https://www.nhs.uk/mental-health/feelings-symptoms-behaviours/behaviours/self-harm/
47. Mind self-harm. https://www.mind.org.uk/information-support/types-of-mental-health-problems/self-harm/helping-yourself-now/
48. NSPCC self-harm. https://www.nspcc.org.uk/keeping-children-safe/childrens-mental-health/self-harm/
49. Action for children self harm. https://parents.actionforchildren.org.uk/mental-health-wellbeing/low-mood-depression/my-child-is-self-harming/
50. Mind self-esteem. https://www.mind.org.uk/information-support/types-of-mental-health-problems/self-esteem/about-self-esteem/
51. Selective mutism information and research association. http://www.selectivemutism.org.uk/
52. Grimmer, T. & Geens, W. (2022) *Nurturing self regulation in early childhood: Adopting an ethos and approach*. Abingdon: Routledge.
53. Mainstone-Cotton, S. (2017) *Promoting emotional wellbeing in early years staff: A practical guide for yourself and your colleagues*. London: Jessica Kingsley Publishers.
54. Taha Wairua. https://anyquestions.govt.nz/many-answers/health-and-well-being-hauora
55. Brene Brown podcast.-https://brenebrown.com/podcast/brene-with-emily-and-amelia-nagoski-on-burnout-and-how-to-complete-the-stress-cycle/
56. Siraj, I., Kingston, D. & Melhuish, E. (2024) *The sustained share thinking and emotional wellbeing scale (SSTEW) scale*. Abingdon: Routledge.
57. Early years TV. https://www.kathybrodie.com/resources/the-new-sstew-scale/
58. Thrive website. https://www.thriveapproach.com/
59. Murphy, K. & Benham, F. (2023) *50 fantastic ideas for supporting neurodiversity*. London: Featherstone.
60. Mainstone-Cotton, S. (2020) *Supporting children through change and everyday transitions: Practical strategies for practitioners and parents*. London: Jessica Kingsley Publishers.

61. Dan Siegel. https://drdansiegel.com/
62. NHS Hampshire child and adolescent service. www.youtube.com/watch?v=K1ovJu2GNVo

Section 2

63. Unicef. https://www.unicef.org.uk/what-we-do/un-convention-child-rights/
64. Unicef. https://www.unicef.org/child-rights-convention/implementing-monitoring
65. Unicef. https://www.unicef.org/child-rights-convention/convention-text-childrens-version
66. Unicef (2002) *For every child*. London: Red Fox.
67. Daniel, V. (2023) *Anti-racist practice in the early years*. Abingdon: Routledge.
68. Murphy, K. (2022) *Supporting the wellbeing of children with SEND*. Abingdon: Routledge
69. Ephgrave, A. (2018) *Planning in the moment with young children: A practical guide for early years practitioners and parents*. Abingdon: Routledge.
70. Joseph Rowntree Foundation. https://www.jrf.org.uk/report/destitution-uk-2023
71. Grimmer, T. (2021) *Developing a loving pedagogy in the early years*. Abingdon: Routledge.
72. National Autistic Society. https://www.autism.org.uk/advice-and-guidance/topics/communication/communication-tools/social-stories-and-comic-strip-coversations#H2_4
73. Elfer, P. & Goldschmied, E. (2011) *Key person in the early years: building relationships for quality provision in early years settings and primary schools*. Abingdon: Routledge.
74. Daniel, V. (2023) *Anti racist practice in the early years*. Abingdon: Routledge.
75. Orchard toys. https://www.orchardtoys.com/
76. Mind. https://www.mind.org.uk/

77. Zoe. https://zoe.com/learn/does-gut-health-affect-mental-health
78. Zoe. https://zoe.com/learn/30-plants-per-week
79. Greenbelt. https://www.greenbelt.org.uk/talks/in-conversation-with-jack-monroe/
80. Sleep foundation. https://www.sleepfoundation.org/how-sleep-works/how-much-sleep-do-we-really-need
81. Balance. https://www.balance-menopause.com/
82. Smiling mind. https://www.smilingmind.com.au/
83. Max Richter. https://www.maxrichtermusic.com/albums/sleep/
84. Fitbit. https://www.fitbit.com/global/uk/home
85. Miyazaki, Y. (2018) *Walking in the woods*. London Aster.
86. BBC. https://www.bbc.co.uk/news/uk-england-derbyshire-64116268
87. Woodland trust. https://www.woodlandtrust.org.uk/visiting-woods/things-to-do/foraging/
88. Outdoor swimmer. https://outdoorswimmer.com/featured/a-beginners-guide-to-wild-swimming/
89. Kristin Neff Ted talk. www.youtube.com/watch?v=IvtZBUSplr4
90. Advent calendar. https://www.myadvent.net/en/
91. Yoga with Adriene. https://yogawithadriene.com/
92. Brene Brown joy and gratitude. www.youtube.com/watch?v=2ljSHUc7TXM
93. Smith, J. (2022) *Why has nobody told me this before*. London: Penguin.
94. The Guardian. https://www.theguardian.com/lifeandstyle/2023/jan/03/52-acts-of-kindness-how-to-spread-joy-in-every-week-of-2023
95. Random acts of kindness. https://www.randomactsofkindness.org/
96. Carly-Campbell, J. & Mainstone-Cotton, S. (2023) *Building positive relationship in the early years*. Abingdon: Routledge.
97. Mind. https://www.mind.org.uk/information-support/local-minds/
98. Cruse. https://www.cruse.org.uk/get-support/
99. Bereavement advice centre. https://www.bereavementadvice.org/topics/coping-with-grief-and-bereavement-advice/useful-contacts/
100. Child outcomes research consortium. https://www.corc.uk.net/news-and-blogs/wellbeing-measurement-for-early-years-staff-survey/
101. Anna Freud. https://www.annafreud.org/resources/under-fives-wellbeing/early-years-staff-wellbeing-a-resource-for-managers-and-teams/
102. Kate Moxley. https://katemoxleyeyc.co.uk/

103. ACAS. https://www.acas.org.uk/supporting-mental-health-workplace/managing-your-employees-mental-health-at-work
104. Mind. https://www.mind.org.uk/workplace/mental-health-at-work/
105. Mind. https://www.mind.org.uk/workplace/mental-health-at-work/taking-care-of-your-staff/
106. Anna Freud. https://www.annafreud.org/
107. GOV.UK. https://help-for-early-years-providers.education.gov.uk/get-help-to-improve-your-practice/early-years-practitioner-wellbeing-support
108. NHS. https://www.nhs.uk/every-mind-matters/
109. Hub of hope. https://hubofhope.co.uk/
110. Mind. https://www.mind.org.uk/workplace/mind-training/
111. Mental health first aid. https://www.mentalhealthfirstaid.org/
112. Anna Freud. https://www.annafreud.org/training/
113. Early education. https://early-education.org.uk/
114. Early years TV. https://www.earlyyears.tv/
115. Kinderly. https://kinderly.co.uk/
116. Parenta. https://www.parenta.com/
117. Family. https://www.famly.co/
118. Sonia Mainstone-Cotton. https://www.soniamainstone-cotton.com/

Index

Note: Page numbers in *italic* indicate a figure on the corresponding page.

T - #0254 - 270225 - C142 - 210/148/7 - PB - 9781032692838 - Matt Lamination